Illicit Trade

Dangerous Fakes

TRADE IN COUNTERFEIT GOODS THAT POSE HEALTH, SAFETY AND ENVIRONMENTAL RISKS

This document reproduces a report jointly prepared by the OECD and the European Union Intellectual Property Office, approved by the OECD's Public Governance Committee by written procedure on 9 March 2022, and prepared for publication by the OECD Secretariat. The opinions expressed and arguments employed herein do not necessarily reflect the official views of all Member States of the European Union.

This document, as well as any data and map included herein, are without prejudice to the status of or sovereignty over any territory, to the delimitation of international frontiers and boundaries and to the name of any territory, city or area.

The names of countries and territories and territorial disclaimers used in this joint publication follow the practice of the OECD.

Note by Turkey
The information in this document with reference to "Cyprus" relates to the southern part of the Island. There is no single authority representing both Turkish and Greek Cypriot people on the Island. Turkey recognises the Turkish Republic of Northern Cyprus (TRNC). Until a lasting and equitable solution is found within the context of the United Nations, Turkey shall preserve its position concerning the "Cyprus issue".

Note by all the European Union Member States of the OECD and the European Union
The Republic of Cyprus is recognised by all members of the United Nations with the exception of Turkey. The information in this document relates to the area under the effective control of the Government of the Republic of Cyprus.

Please cite this publication as:
OECD/EUIPO (2022), *Dangerous Fakes: Trade in Counterfeit Goods that Pose Health, Safety and Environmental Risks*, Illicit Trade, OECD Publishing, Paris, https://doi.org/10.1787/117e352b-en.

ISBN 978-92-64-34676-5 (print)
ISBN 978-92-64-59470-8 (pdf)
ISBN 978-92-64-76020-2 (HTML)
ISBN 978-92-64-89721-2 (epub)

Illicit Trade
ISSN 2617-5827 (print)
ISSN 2617-5835 (online)

European Union
ISBN:
978-92-9156-314-2 (print)
978-92-9156-313-5 (pdf)
978-92-9156-316-6 (HTML)
978-92-9156-315-9 (epub)
Catalogue number:
TB-06-22-156-EN-C (print)
TB-06-22-156-EN-N (pdf)
TB-06-22-156-EN-Q (HTML)
TB-06-22-156-EN-E (epub)

Photo credits: Cover © Roman Krause.

Corrigenda to publications may be found on line at: www.oecd.org/about/publishing/corrigenda.htm.
© OECD/EUIPO 2022

The use of this work, whether digital or print, is governed by the Terms and Conditions to be found at https://www.oecd.org/termsandconditions.

Preface

Illicit trade in counterfeit and pirated goods poses a major challenge to a global economy. It is dangerous for consumers, damages economic growth and fuels organised crime, which can undermine trust in functioning markets and the rule of law. The COVID-19 pandemic has exacerbated existing problems by re-shaping value chains, shifting consumer demand, and, consequently, opening new opportunities for illicit trade networks. At the same time, illicit trade creates significant additional risks to consumers, including health, safety and environmental risks. Policy makers need solid empirical evidence to take action against this threat. To meet this need, the OECD and the EU Intellectual Property Office (EUIPO) have long joined forces to carry out a series of analytical studies. The results have been published in a set of reports that gauge illicit trade in counterfeit and pirated goods.

We are very pleased to provide a unique insight to the illicit trade in fake goods that pose health, safety and environmental threats. We are confident that the results will enhance our understanding of the risks that counterfeiting poses to the global economy and society, facilitate the development of innovative policy options to respond to these challenges, and promote clean trade in the COVID-19 recovery.

Christian Archambeau,
Executive Director,
EUIPO

Elsa Pilichowski,
Director of the Public Governance Directorate,
OECD

Foreword

Illicit trade in fake goods is a significant and growing threat in a globalised economy. Its harmful impact on consumers, economic growth, innovation, the rule of law and, ultimately, trust in well-functioning global markets should not be underestimated.

In recent years, the OECD and the EU Intellectual Property Office (EUIPO) have been collecting evidence on various aspects of this risk. The results have been published in a set of reports starting with *Trade in Counterfeit and Pirated Goods: Mapping the Economic Impact* (2016). These results have since been expanded and updated in subsequent reports, including *Trends in Trade in Counterfeit and Pirated Goods* (2019) and *Global Trade in Fakes: A Worrying Trend* (2021). The results are a major concern, as trade in counterfeit and pirated goods amounted to up to 2.5 % of world trade in 2019; when considering only imports into the EU, fake goods amounted to up to 5.8 % of imports. These amounts are similar to those of previous years, and illicit trade in fakes remains a serious risk to modern, open and globalised economies.

Trade in counterfeit goods is a major risk for today's modern, productive and forward-looking global economy. It not only strikes at the heart of the engine of sustainable economic growth, but also poses significant risks to health, safety and the environment.

This report builds on previous analysis, presenting detailed, quantitative information on the value of illicit trade in fake goods that can pose health risks (e.g. fake pharmaceuticals or food products), safety risks (e.g. counterfeit automotive spare parts, fake batteries) and environmental risks (e.g. fake chemicals or pesticides). The evidence in this report can help raise awareness of the risks of this trade and its implications for health and environmental policy.

This study was carried out under the auspices of the OECD's Task Force on Countering Illicit Trade, which focuses on evidence-based research and advanced analytics to assist policy makers in mapping and understanding the vulnerabilities exploited and created by illicit trade. This report was approved by the Public Governance Committee via written procedure on 9 March and prepared for publication by the OECD Secretariat.

Acknowledgements

This report was prepared by the OECD Public Governance Directorate, under the leadership of Elsa Pilichowski, Public Governance Director and Martin Forst, Head of the Governance Reviews and Partnerships division, together with the European Observatory on Infringements of Intellectual Property Rights, led by its Director Paul Maier, at the the European Union Intellectual Property Office (EUIPO).

At the OECD this study was conducted under the auspices of the Task Force on Countering Illicit Trade (TF-CIT). It was shared with other OECD committees with relevant expertise in the areas of trade, regulatory policy, consumer protection policy, product safety and public sector integrity.

The report was prepared by Piotr Stryszowski, Senior Economist and Morgane Gaudiau, Economist at the OECD Directorate for Public Governance jointly with Michał Kazimierczak, Economist at the European Observatory on Infringements of Intellectual Property Rights of the EUIPO and Nathan Wajsman, Chief Economist, EUIPO. Peter Avery, Senior Consultant provided valuable inputs. The authors wish to thank the OECD experts who provided valuable knowledge and insights: János Bertok, Julio Bacio Terracino, and Nick Malyshev from the OECD Public Governance Directorate, Silvia Sorescu from the OECD Trade Directorate and Brigitte Acoca and Nicholas McSpedden-Brown from the OECD Directorate for Science, Technology and Innovation.

The authors would also like to thank experts from the OECD member countries and participants of several seminars and workshops for their valuable assistance. Special expressions of appreciation are given to Kerry Manion from the US Food and Drug Administration and to Sergio Tirro, Monica De Astis and Aikaterini Giannelou from Europol.

Kevin Mushi served as a research assistant and Ciara Muller and Andrea Uhrhammer provided editorial and production support.

The database on customs seizures was provided by the World Customs Organization (WCO) and supplemented with regional data submitted by the European Commission's Directorate-General for Taxation and Customs Union, the US Customs and Border Protection Agency and the US Immigration and Customs Enforcement. The authors express their gratitude for the data and for the valuable support of these institutions.

Table of contents

Preface — 3

Foreword — 4

Acknowledgements — 5

Executive Summary — 9

Introduction — 11

1 Which Fakes are more likely to be Dangerous? — 13
    Product safety requirements, norms and standards — 14
    Product recalls and alerts — 17

2 Dangerous Products – Types of Risks — 22
    Effects on health — 22
    Effects on safety — 25
    Environmental impact — 32
    Personal security — 34

3 Trade in Potential Dangerous Counterfeit Products – Quantitative Analysis — 36
    The broad scope — 36
    EU Case Study — 47
    Focused scope — 50
    EU Case Study — 62
    Industry focuses — 68

4 Concluding Remarks — 73
    Next steps — 74

Annex A. Methodological notes — 76
    A.1. Constructing the General Trade-Related Index of Counterfeiting for products (GTRIC-p) — 76
    A.2. Constructing the general trade-related index of counterfeiting economies (GTRIC-e) — 78
    A.3. Constructing the General Trade-Related Index of Counterfeiting (GTRIC) — 80
    A.4. Calculating the absolute value — 81

References — 83

Tables

Table 1.1. Counterfeit products with health and safety implications 16
Table 1.2. Product recalls contained in the OECD's GlobalRecalls portal, 2019-21 17
Table 1.3. FDA product recalls, withdrawals and safety alerts, 2019-2021 18
Table 1.4. NHSTA recalls and safety issues, 2019-21 18
Table 1.5. Risk table 20
Table 1.6. Counterfeit products with health and safety implications 21
Table 2.1. Examples of unauthorized use of UL mark during 2020-22 26

Figures

Figure 3.1. Main product categories of dangerous goods subject to counterfeiting, 2017-19 38
Figure 3.2. Main provenance economies of dangerous fakes, 2017-19 38
Figure 3.3. Main destination economies of dangerous fakes, 2017-19 39
Figure 3.4. Conveyance methods of dangerous goods subject to counterfeiting, 2017-19 40
Figure 3.5. Main product categories of dangerous fakes shipped by vessel, 2017-19 40
Figure 3.6. Main provenance economies of dangerous fakes shipped by vessel, 2017-19 41
Figure 3.7. Main destination economies of dangerous fakes shipped by vessel, 2017-19 42
Figure 3.8. Main provenance destination economies of the most frequently counterfeit dangerous goods (toys building set) shipped by vessel, 2017-19 42
Figure 3.9. Shipment size of the most frequently faked product (building set) shipped by vessel, 2017-19 43
Figure 3.10. Shipment size of dangerous goods subject to counterfeiting, 2017-19 43
Figure 3.11. Main product categories of small parcels of dangerous fakes, 2017-19 44
Figure 3.12. Main provenance economies of small parcels of dangerous fakes, 2017-19 45
Figure 3.13. Main destination economies of small parcels of dangerous fakes, 2017-19 45
Figure 3.14. Main provenance-destination economies of the most frequently faked dangerous good (sports shoes) shipped through small parcel, 2017-19 46
Figure 3.15. Conveyance methods of the most frequently faked dangerous good (sneaker) shipped through small parcel, 2017-19 46
Figure 3.16. Main product categories of dangerous counterfeit goods imported into the EU, 2017-19 47
Figure 3.17. Main destination economies of dangerous counterfeit goods imported into the EU, 2017-19 48
Figure 3.18. Main provenance economies of dangerous counterfeit goods imported into the EU, 2017-19 48
Figure 3.19. Conveyance methods of dangerous counterfeit goods imported into the EU, 2017-19 49
Figure 3.20. Shipment size of dangerous counterfeit goods imported into the EU, 2017-19 50
Figure 3.21. Estimates of global trade in dangerous fakes, 2017-19 52
Figure 3.22. Main provenance economies of dangerous fakes, 2017-19 53
Figure 3.23. Main destination economies of dangerous fakes, 2017-19 53
Figure 3.24. Main dangerous product categories subject to counterfeiting, 2017-19 54
Figure 3.25. Conveyance methods of dangerous goods subject to counterfeiting, 2017-19 55
Figure 3.26. Main product categories of dangerous fake goods shipped by vessel, 2017-19 55
Figure 3.27. Main provenance economies of dangerous fake goods shipped by vessel, 2017-19 56
Figure 3.28. Main destination economies of dangerous fake goods shipped by vessel, 2017-19 57
Figure 3.29. Shipment size of dangerous goods seized, 2017-19 57
Figure 3.30. Main product categories of small parcels of dangerous fakes, 2017-19 58
Figure 3.31. Main provenance economies of small parcels of dangerous fakes, 2017-19 59
Figure 3.32. Main destination economies of small parcels of dangerous fakes, 2017-19 59
Figure 3.33. Transport mode of small parcels of dangerous fakes, 2017-19 60
Figure 3.34. Main provenance-destination economies of the most frequently faked product (perfumes) sent via small parcels, 2017-19 61
Figure 3.35. Transport modes of the most frequently faked product (perfumes) sent via small parcels, 2017-19 61
Figure 3.36. Main product categories of dangerous fakes seized destined to the EU, 2017-19 62
Figure 3.37. Main provenance economies of dangerous fakes seized destined to the EU, 2017-19 63
Figure 3.38. Main destination economies of dangerous fakes seized destined to the EU, 2017-19 63
Figure 3.39. Conveyance methods of dangerous fakes subject to counterfeiting imported into the EU, 2017-19 64
Figure 3.40. Shipment size of dangerous goods seized imported into the EU, 2017-19 64
Figure 3.41. Distribution of online and offline sales among dangerous fakes destined to the EU, 2017-19 65
Figure 3.42. Product categories of dangerous fakes purchased online, 2017-19 66
Figure 3.43. Provenance economies of dangerous fakes purchased online, 2017-19 66

Figure 3.44. Provenance economies of dangerous fakes purchased on site, 2017-19	67
Figure 3.45. Modes of transport of dangerous fakes purchased on site (left) and online (right), 2017-19, in terms of number of global customs seizures	67
Figure 3.46. Main provenance economies of counterfeit foodstuffs, 2017-19	68
Figure 3.47. Main destination economies of counterfeit foodstuffs, 2017-19	69
Figure 3.48. Transport modes used to ship counterfeit foodstuffs, 2017-19	69
Figure 3.49. Shipments size of counterfeit food products, 2017-19	70
Figure 3.50. Top provenance economies for counterfeit perfumery and cosmetics, 2017-19	70
Figure 3.51. Top destination economies for counterfeit perfumery and cosmetics, 2017-19	71
Figure 3.52. Conveyance methods used to ship counterfeit perfumery and cosmetics, 2017-19	71
Figure 3.53. Shipment size of counterfeit perfumery and cosmetics, 2017-19	72

Boxes

Box 1.1. EU definition of safe products	19
Box 2.1. Examples of methanol poisoning	24
Box 2.2. CPSC safety alert on hoverboards, 2017	28
Box 2.3. Lithium battery safety concerns	29
Box 2.4. Street sales of counterfeit Microsoft software	35

Follow OECD Publications on:

 http://twitter.com/OECD_Pubs

 http://www.facebook.com/OECDPublications

 http://www.linkedin.com/groups/OECD-Publications-4645871

 http://www.youtube.com/oecdilibrary

 http://www.oecd.org/oecddirect/

Executive Summary

This study quantitatively assesses the scope and trends of the trade in counterfeit products that pose health, safety and environmental threats. It is based on an analysis of a unique international set of customs seizure data and other enforcement data, combined with structured interviews with enforcement experts.

In principle, all counterfeit goods are risky and can pose some threats to users. To take into account different degrees of risk, the study introduces two specific approaches to determine the scope of dangerous fakes.

The broad approach considers the goods that need to meet product specific safety standards and/or are under the scope of the US Food and Drugs Administration and/or are subject of the draft United States bill – the SHOP SAFE ACT. Using this approach, one finds that apparel products, automotive spare parts, optical and medical apparatuses, as well as pharmaceuticals are the most frequently occurring dangerous counterfeits.

China and Hong Kong (China) are the largest identified exporters of dangerous fakes, accounting for more than three-quarters of seizures. Postal parcels – driven by the rising popularity of e-commerce – are the most common method of shipping dangerous fakes, significantly complicating screening and detection processes and lowering the risk of detection and penalties. The European Union and the United States were the main destination economies of the small parcels containing dangerous goods. However, in terms of the value of seizures, shipments by sea cargo clearly dominate. The distribution of destinations of dangerous fakes shipped by sea varied, with Arabian Gulf countries at the top of the list.

A more focused, narrow approach looks only at foodstuffs, pharmaceuticals, cosmetics and goods' categories that have been most frequently subject of safety alerts and recalls. This approach reveals that the most commonly traded product categories of dangerous fakes were perfumery and cosmetics, clothing, toys, automotive spare parts and pharmaceuticals. Most of these goods originated in China (55% of global customs seizures) and Hong Kong (China) (19%). 60% of dangerous goods seized were shipped by postal services, while sea was the dominant transport mode in terms of seized value.

Online sales represented 60% of global seizures of dangerous products destined for the EU. In terms of seized value, they represented only a small share, however. Among dangerous fakes ordered online cosmetics items were the most common, followed by clothing, toys and automotive spare parts. Most of these goods (75%) were shipped from China.

The COVID-19 pandemic has affected trade in dangerous fake goods, and, in most cases, the crisis has aggravated existing trends. This is particularly the case for counterfeit medicines, and other high-risk sectors such as alcohol, where broken supply chains and shifting demand created new potential for criminal activity. However, this overall sharp increase in fakes concerned not only medicines and personal protective equipment (PPE), but many other goods that can also pose health and safety risks, including consumer goods and spare parts.

To understand and combat the risk posed by the trade in dangerous counterfeit and pirated goods, governments need up-to-date information on its magnitude, scope and trends. This study is part of a continuous monitoring effort to support policy formulation and enforcement.

Introduction

Existing quantitative analysis of illicit trade in counterfeit and pirated goods indicates that the range of products that are subject of counterfeiting is very broad and keeps widening (OECD/EUIPO, 2021b[1]). Any product for which intellectual property (IP) adds economic value to rights holders becomes a target for counterfeiters; the counterfeiting thus affects not only luxury goods, but also intermediate products and a wide range of common consumer products. For all these goods counterfeits cause economic damage by destroying jobs, stealing profits and lowering innovation incentives.

At the same time, for some products, counterfeits are often of low quality, which creates significant risks for consumers. These include health risks (e.g. fake pharmaceuticals, toys or food products), safety risks (e.g. fake automotive spare parts, fake batteries) and environmental risks (e.g. fake chemicals or pesticides). For all these products, legitimate suppliers must comply with health, safety or environmental regulations to make sure their products will cause no harm or damage. Counterfeiters are not bound by these regulations and consequently, the fake goods that they offer can pose significant health, safety and environmental risks.

In addition to damaging health and safety risks, counterfeiting has wide-ranging damaging economic effects. The OECD and EUIPO have already carried out a study on counterfeiting and piracy in the pharmaceutical sector which documents the damaging effects on economies. This study complements the work that has been done, with follow up analysis that looks at the health, safety and environmental risks posed by fakes in a number of sectors including food products and personal protective equipment, where fakes are often substandard and are stored and transported in poor conditions, which can pose serious health risks to consumers. The study also looks at toys and batteries, where fakes are sometimes produced without observing any safety norms, and hence can pose significant hazards. Lastly, it looks at chemicals and pesticides, where fake products which are not in accordance with environmental regulations can lead to significant environmental damage.

Measuring the magnitude and scope of counterfeiting is in general difficult due to the clandestine nature of this phenomenon. While major progress has been made on measuring its prevalence in international trade, as the result of the econometric work carried out by the OECD and EUIPO, work on the dangers posed by counterfeit products is lacking, relying predominantly on anecdotal information.

This study carries out an in-depth analysis of counterfeiting and piracy for a range of goods with elevated health safety or environmental risks. It provides detailed information on the value of counterfeit trade in such goods, including analysis of the volumes and composition of these products. The report maps the key trade routes used to distribute the fake products and also examines the different types of health and safety risks caused by counterfeits.

The analysis is carried out in two steps.

The first step determines the types of products which are most prone to causing health, safety and environmental risks. It i) describes the methodologies employed by governments to assess the potential risks a product can pose to consumers (i.e. whether or not they are counterfeit), ii) examines the harm that substandard counterfeit products has actually caused to consumers across a broad range of products, iii) describes how adulterated counterfeit products, in particular software, can seriously undermine personal security, iv) assesses the damaging effects that counterfeit products have on the environment and v) reviews the types of genuine products that have been subject to recalls and safety alerts, as revealed in public databases, as those products which are most frequently subject to recalls may also be those for which counterfeit products pose particular risks.

The second step relies on the GTRIC methodology (see Annex A) developed for previous EUIPO/OECD studies. This methodology is applied to develop an estimation of total value of counterfeit trade in fakes that pose health, safety or environmental risks, and is then used to develop a mapping of key trade routes of these products, from production points to the destination markets (including modes of transports and intermediary points). Evidence of the modes of transport abused in trade of such goods is also explored.

The quantitative analysis is based on the period before the COVID-19 pandemic. The pandemic has significantly reshaped both licit trade and trade in counterfeit goods, however given the fast pace of changes, a precise quantitative analysis of these effects has not yet been possible.

In summary, this study sheds light on trade in unsafe fake goods posing health, safety or environmental risks. Individual concerns about possible negative health and safety risks related to consumption of counterfeits can affect demand for counterfeits. In fact, existing studies suggest that individual health and safety concerns are very effective deterrents for consumers who consider purchasing counterfeit products. However, as shown in EUIPO's study "European Citizens and Intellectual Property: Perception, Awareness and Behaviour", very often consumers are unaware that they are buying a counterfeit. Hence, robust, and complete information about the health and safety risks posed by counterfeits could feed into effective awareness campaigns, and consequently reduce demand for fakes. Consequently, the study could be used by policymakers in developing awareness campaigns, and could enhance understanding of the need for including anti-counterfeiting elements in shaping health policies, environmental policies.

1 Which Fakes are more likely to be Dangerous?

Ensuring that products available on markets are safe is a keen concern of governments, which have set up legislation and created regulatory bodies to oversee markets and identify unsafe, or dangerous, products. In many countries, responsibility for the market oversight is assigned to multiple agencies, with each covering different sets of products. Food and drugs, for example, are sometimes treated by one agency while automotive and other consumer products are treated by others. When dangerous products are detected, they are generally subject to recalls or other measures to eliminate the potential risk to consumers.

The agencies responsible for overseeing product safety generally focus on the safety requirements of the products, without specifically focusing on the counterfeit angle. Counterfeit items raise important challenges as they masquerade as genuine products but are not subject to the same production scrutiny; they therefore free ride on the performance and testing done on the genuine products. While the genuine products may be considered safe, the counterfeit items might thus have undetected defects that raise health and safety concerns. Overall, US authorities have deemed automotive parts, electronics, safety equipment, prescription drugs, and cosmetics as the most dangerous counterfeits due to the potential threats they present to public safety and health.[1] EUIPO found in its qualitative study on risks posed by counterfeits to consumers that in particular goods aimed at children could present serious risks when they are counterfeited, including toys, childcare items and children's clothing[2].

As noted above, genuine products can also pose health, safety and environmental threats, which is why regulatory bodies are actively engaged in market surveillance. While, in general products may be considered safe when they are manufactured, subsequent handling can pose problems. This can happen for example, if goods are illicitly diverted outside legitimate supply chains, and are subsequently improperly stored or transported. For instance, medicines often require transport and storage in special, temperature-controlled conditions in order to maintain their therapeutic value.

Apart from pharmaceuticals, many other products can pose health, safety and environmental risks, even when they do not necessarily violate IP rights. These would include for example substandard goods that fail to meet either quality standards or specifications, or both. It also includes unregistered or unlicensed products that have not undergone evaluation and/or approval by national or regional regulatory authorities for the market in which they are marketed/distributed or used. As an interviewed enforcement officer noted "Counterfeit products are just a sea on a big ocean of dangerous products". This study takes note of the broad scope of potentially dangerous counterfeit products, using existing concepts.

Two important issues should be kept in mind in the context of the scope of the study.

First, even though counterfeit products are often substandard, it is not their quality that determines whether or not they are counterfeit. In fact, some counterfeit goods may seem to be of good quality, although interviews with enforcement and industry experts indicate such cases are rare.

Second, counterfeits have a variety of socio-economic effects on economies, threatening legitimate businesses, governments, consumers and the society as a whole (OECD/EUIPO, 2016[2]); (OECD/EUIPO,

2019[3]), (OECD/EUIPO, 2021b[1]). This study focuses on health, safety and environmental risks posed by such goods, which is only a subset of the overall threat posed by counterfeits.

To establish the scope of counterfeits that can pose health, safety or environmental harm one can take several approaches.

- One looks at all products that need to meet product specific health and safety standard, before entering the market.
- A more narrow approach, looks at specific product recalls and alerts, and identify the product categories that were most frequently subject of such safety incidents.

Due to lack of systematic checks of actual safety, health and environmental risks of seized counterfeit products, the available information is scarce and based only on anecdotal evidence. Notably, it is not sufficient for carrying out the actual risk analysis for the broad set of counterfeit products available in the seizures data. The main assumption in this report is therefore that counterfeit products are less likely to meet the product specific health, safety and environmental standards than the goods put on the market by the original rights' holders and therefore they pose greater safety risks. Further to this assumption, the term counterfeit dangerous goods should be understood as referring to the counterfeits:

- in those products' categories that need to meet product specific safety standards and/or are under the scope of the US Food and Drugs Administration and/or are subject of the draft United States bill – the SHOP SAFE ACT (the broad scope);
- in product categories of foodstuffs, pharmaceuticals, cosmetics and categories that are most frequently subject of safety incidents as evidenced by product recalls and alerts (the focused scope).

Product safety requirements, norms and standards

As noted above, to ensure the free movement and safety of products in the EU, the New Legislative Framework (NLF)[3], as the general framework for EU product legislation in the non-food area, was adopted in 2008. The NLF was built on the New Approach, which restricted the content of legislation to "essential requirements" leaving the technical details to European harmonised standards. Products manufactured in compliance with harmonised standards benefit from a presumption of conformity with the corresponding essential requirements of the applicable legislation.

Regulation (EC) No 765/2008 established the legal basis for accreditation and market surveillance and consolidated the meaning of the CE marking, thus filling an existing void. This Regulation is partially replaced by the new Market Surveillance Regulation[4]. Decision No 768/2008/EC sets up a model to be used in preparing and revising Union harmonisation legislation with the aim to update, harmonise and consolidate the various technical instruments already used in existing Union harmonisation legislation: definitions, criteria for the designation and notification of conformity assessment bodies, rules for the notification process, the conformity assessment procedures (modules) and the rules for their use, the safeguard mechanisms, the obligations of the economic operators and traceability requirements. More than 20 pieces of Union legislation are aligned today with the NLF[5].

In line with the OECD Recommendation on Consumer Product Safety[6], in some jurisdictions a general safety requirement is provided for in legislation, mandating all products placed on the market to be safe, indistinctly of whether they infringe an intellectual property right or not[7]. Standards can be developed by industry or standardisation bodies and applicable to a given product

The goal of this study is to determine the potential scope of products with elevated risks, not to present an exhaustive list of the agencies which are involved and the challenges they are facing in identifying dangerous products. Consequently, this section will look only at few areas of governance efforts, namely:

- Harmonization of product quality standardization in the European Union.
- The activities of the US Food and Drug Administration.
- Discussion in the United States surrounding the SHOP SAFE Act.

Harmonised standards in the EU

The safety of products placed on the EU market is regulated by the General Product Safety Directive and specific provisions of the European Union legislation harmonising the conditions for the marketing of products (European Union harmonisation legislation). The General Product Safety Directive sets out a general product safety requirement, applicable to all products and risks not covered by specific harmonisation legislation. The General Product Safety and Union harmonisation legislation provide for the establishment of European standards cited in the Official Journal of the EU, granting a presumption of safety to products complying with them. These are European standards developed by a recognised European Standards Organisation: CEN (European Committee for Standardization), CENELEC (European Committee for Electrotechnical Standardization), or ETSI (European Telecommunications Standards Institute). These standards are drafted following a request from the European Commission to one of these organisations. Manufacturers, other economic operators, or conformity assessment bodies can use harmonised standards to demonstrate that products, services, or processes comply with relevant EU legislation.

The CE marking indicates that a product has been successfully assessed to meet safety, health, and environmental protection requirements. Products that require CE marking must undergo quality checks (by the economic operator or in some cases by a third party) and must necessarily be marked with the CE logo prior to entering the European market. This includes such goods as machinery, toys, electrical equipment, medical devices and construction products[8].

In the EU context, apart from the Harmonized Products system, the work carried out by EU agencies such as ECHA (European Chemicals Agency), EMA (European Medicines Agency) and EFSA (European Foods Safety Agency) is particularly relevant to understanding the risks associated with chemical, medicinal and food products.

US Food and Drug Administration (FDA)

The FDA is responsible for regulating food products, cosmetics and pharmaceuticals that can pose health and safety risks.

While the specific programs for safety regulation carried out by the FDA vary widely by the type of product, the common focus is the potential risks entailed by the goods. The FDA is responsible for protecting and promoting public health, and hence, the scope of its work is a good indication of goods that, if counterfeited, could pose significant health, safety and environmental risks to consumers.

The FDA focus is on food products, dietary supplements, prescription and over-the-counter pharmaceutical medications, vaccines, biopharmaceuticals, medical devices, cosmetics, animal foods and feed, and veterinary products.

In some areas, where possible risks can be pronounced, FDA regulation is far-reaching. For example, for prescription drugs, FDA's regulation deals with testing, manufacturing, labelling, advertising, marketing, efficacy, and safety issues. The most rigorous requirements apply to new molecular entities (i.e. drugs that are not based on existing medications). For other products, such as cosmetics, regulation can be less restrictive, focusing on the accuracy of information on labelling and on the product safety.

US SHOP SAFE Act of 2021

Under the proposed US SHOP SAFE Act, an electronic commerce platform would, in certain circumstances be liable for infringement of a registered trademark by a third-party seller of goods when those goods implicate the health and safety of consumers.[9] The Act further defines the goods concerned as:

> "… goods the use of which can lead to illness, disease, injury, serious adverse event, allergic reaction, or death if produced without compliance with all applicable Federal, State, and local health and safety regulations and industry-designated testing, safety, quality, certification, manufacturing, packaging, and labelling standards."

The scope of the products that would be covered under the legislation was addressed at a May 2021 hearing on the bill, and in a number of written submissions to the House Judiciary Committee on the 2021 bill, as well its 2020 precursor.[10] A group of associations representing a broad range of product sectors[11] submitted a joint letter that endorses the emphasis on consumer health and safety as a priority, while arguing that a broader scope that would take other adverse effects on the economy would be beneficial.[12] In a separate filing, the Transnational Association to Combat Illicit Trade (TRACIT) suggested that legislation should avoid creating categories that may ultimately require the judicial system to establish parameters around the vague concept of "safety and health."[13] Table 1.1 summarizes a list of products coined during the discussion on the Act.

Table 1.1. Counterfeit products with health and safety implications

(list made during the public debates on the US SHOP SAFE Act)

Product	Associated risks
Beauty products	Bacterial contamination; inadequate or missing preservative systems; toxic/hazardous ingredients (chemical and biological hazards, heavy metals); non-disclosed or high levels of allergens; presence of banned ingredients; presence of mold; absence or decreased levels of drug and/or sanitizing/disinfectant active ingredients; electrical and/or burn hazards.
Disinfecting/sanitizing products	
Feminine care products	
Food and beverages	
Medicines	
Oral care products	
Pet products	
Children's products	Noncompliance with safety standards; toxic/hazardous/flammable ingredients.
Cleaning/laundry products	Toxic/hazardous/banned ingredients.
Construction products	Fire/electrical hazards; critical engineering failures.
Digital/communication products, replacement parts/equipment or networks	Fire/electrical hazards; noncompliance with manufacturing/safety standards; failure at critical moments.
Electrical appliances/equipment and replacement parts	Noncompliance with manufacturing/safety standards; fire/electrical hazards; toxic/hazardous chemicals.
Furniture	Noncompliance with manufacturing/safety standards; toxic/hazardous/flammable ingredients.
Jewelry, luxury goods, textiles	Allergic reactions; treated with chemicals that can be hazardous, flammable, toxic.
Nicotine containing products	Toxic/hazardous/banned ingredients.
Office supplies	Toxic/hazardous chemicals; equipment damage.
Personal health care equipment, medical devices	Noncompliance with safety standards; fail at critical moments; long term health effects due to toxic/hazardous/flammable ingredients (chemical, biological, bacterial, heavy metals).
Personal protective equipment	
Product packaging	
Pesticides	Toxic/hazardous chemicals; environmental impact.
Sports equipment	Noncompliance with safety standards; fail at critical moments; toxic/hazardous ingredients.
Transportation and replacement parts	Fire hazards; system severely impacted; compromised data transmission of confidential/critical, Personal identifiable, healthcare related, educational, military information.
Documentation	Fraudulent access.

Source: (TRACIT, n.d.[4]).

The Intellectual Property Law Section of the American Bar Association weighed in on the 2020 version of the bill, voicing its support for the legislation, on the presumption that the definition of goods that have implications for the health and safety of consumers would be broadly interpreted.[14] The Section noted the importance of acknowledging that there will be a grey area of goods that do not fall clearly into the category of goods implicating health and safety. Clothing and toys, it is pointed out, are not goods generally presumed to be a threat to the health or safety of consumers, but there are instances when certain clothing might contain harmful chemicals or toys may contain lead or other prohibited chemicals. The scope of the legislation, it is argued, should capture these situations. The risk that some products could be dangerous, however, could, it is pointed out, and result in the need for e-commerce platforms to apply the proposed enhanced practices more broadly to all products to ensure they would not be held liable for contributory infringement.

Product recalls and alerts

Many countries have established databases or information systems for authorities to exchange urgent alerts on dangerous products, which are also notably used to inform interested parties, including consumers, about product safety issues and product recalls. Such databases can be useful for flagging products and product areas where health and safety issues are of particular concern.

OECD GlobalRecalls portal

The OECD has played a major role in bringing the information on recalls together, in a multilingual platform. Its GlobalRecalls portal, launched in 2012, collects information on product recalls being issued around the world, on a regular basis.[15] The database currently contains more than 33,000 notifications, from 47 jurisdictions. More than 15 000 notifications originate from the EU/European Economic Area countries. Where possible, the notifications have been placed in one of 35 product categories. For the years 2019-21, automotive products accounted for the largest share of the notifications, followed by toys and games and electrical supplies (Table 1.2).

Table 1.2. Product recalls contained in the OECD's GlobalRecalls portal, 2019-21

Product group	Number of notifications	Share of total (%)
Automotive	1,436	22
Toys/games	1,233	19
Electrical supplies	693	10
Clothing	480	7
Sports equipment	405	6
Household/office furniture/furnishings	357	5
Beauty/personal care/hygiene	290	4
Personal accessories	273	4
Safety/protection-DIY	153	2
Home appliances	149	2
Plumbing/heating/ventilation/air conditioning	147	2
Healthcare	145	2
Stationery/office machinery/occasion supplies	135	2
Lawn/garden supplies	110	2
Other	599	9
Total	6,605	100

Note: Total including 3,625 notifications which were unclassified.
Source: (OECD, n.d.[5])

The scope of the reported recalls, it should be noted, varies, by jurisdiction. Data for the European Union, for example, which reports for its Member States, does not include food products, nor does US data, which only covers products under the purview of the Consumer Product Safety Commission (CPSC). Similarly, Japan's notifications do not include food products, vehicles and pharmaceuticals (including cosmetics) and Canadian notifications exclude a number of products, including cosmetics, vehicles and drugs. Getting a complete overview of products subject to recalls, thus requires consideration of multiple databases. In the case of the United States, for example, in addition to the database operated by the CPSC, those maintained by the FDA on food and drugs (Table 1.3) and the NHSTA on automotive products (Table 1.4) would need to be consulted to obtain a more complete overview of recalls and safety alerts.

Table 1.3. FDA product recalls, withdrawals and safety alerts, 2019-2021

Product group	Number of notifications	Share of total (%)
Food and beverages	779	63
Drugs	275	22
Animal and veterinary	97	8
Medical devices	46	4
Dietary supplements	33	3
Cosmetics	12	1
Tobacco	2	(1)
Biologics	1	(1)
Total	1,837	100(2)

Notes: (1) Less than 0.5% ; (2) Total does not add due to rounding.
Source: (FDA, n.d.[6]).

Table 1.4. NHSTA recalls and safety issues, 2019-21

Product group	Number of notifications	Share of total (%)
Equipment	505	17
Electrical system	370	13
Service brakes	244	8
Airbags	217	7
Fuel system	183	6
Suspension	177	6
Exterior lighting	175	6
Structure	163	6
Steering	149	5
Power train	136	5
Other	621	21
Total	2,940	100

Source: (NHSTA, n.d.[7]).

EU Rapid Alert System for Dangerous Products (Safety Gate)

Another example of an alert system for unsafe products identified on the market is the EU Rapid Alert System for Dangerous products (Safety Gate), which was established under EU's Directive 2001/95/EC of the European Parliament and of the Council of 3 December 2001 on general product safety (GPSD). The Guidelines for management of this rapid alert system are defined in Commission Implementing Decision (EU) 2019/417.

The directive defines dangerous products indirectly, as any that do not meet its definition of a "safe product" (Box 1.1). When a measure is taken against an unsafe product, Member States are required to issue a notification in a Safety Gate. The notifications distinguish between:[16]

- Measures taken against products posing a serious risk ("Article 12 notification");
- Measures taken against products posing a serious risk requiring emergency measures;
- Measures taken against products posing less than serious risk ("Article 11 notification");
- Other notifications ("for information"). These concern other cases falling outside the 3 categories mentioned above, mostly because the information is not complete enough to ensure the required follow up by enforcement network authorities of the Safety Gate network.

Box 1.1. EU definition of safe products

"Safe product" shall mean any product which, under normal or reasonably foreseeable conditions of use including duration and, where applicable, putting into service, installation and maintenance requirements, does not present any risk or only the minimum risks compatible with the product's use, considered to be acceptable and consistent with a high level of protection for the safety and health of persons, taking into account the following points, in particular:

1. the characteristics of the product, including its composition, packaging, instructions for assembly and, where applicable, for installation and maintenance;
2. the effect on other products, where it is reasonably foreseeable that it will be used with other products;
3. the presentation of the product, the labelling, any warnings and instructions for its use and disposal and any other indication or information regarding the product
4. the categories of consumers at risk when using the product, in particular children and the elderly.

Source: Directive 2001/95/EC.

The Commission implementing decision (EU) 2019/417 lays down guidelines for the operation of the rapid alert system Safety Gate. It defines the risk of a product by combining the probability of damage occurring during the lifetime of a product with the severity of a certain injury caused by the product. Severity of injuries is set in 4 levels (1 to 4) and depends on the type of injury at stake. Four categories of risk are established:

- Serious;
- High;
- Medium;
- Low.

This results in the following table that shows the risk level from the combination of the severity of injury and its probability.

Table 1.5. Risk table

Probability of damage during the foreseeable lifetime of a product	Severity of injury			
	1	2	3	4
>50%	High risk	Serious risk	Serious risk	Serious risk
>1/10	Medium risk	Serious risk	Serious risk	Serious risk
>1/100	Medium risk	Serious risk	Serious risk	Serious risk
>1/1,000	Low risk	High risk	Serious risk	Serious risk
>1/10,000	Low risk	Medium risk	High risk	Serious risk
>1/100,000	Low risk	Low risk	Medium risk	High risk
>1/1,000,000	Low risk	Low risk	Low risk	Medium risk
<1/1,000,000	Low risk	Low risk	Low risk	Low risk

Source: Commission Implementing Decision (EU) 2019/417.

Within the Safety Gate notification system, authorities are asked to indicate whether a product subject to a measure is counterfeit, or not. In 2019, the EUIPO conducted a study of the 191 notifications which were flagged as pertaining to counterfeit products during the 2010-17 period (EUIPO, 2019[8]).17 The analysis revealed that:

- Some 97% of recorded dangerous counterfeit goods were assessed as posing a serious risk.
- Toys were the most popular type of product followed by clothing, textiles and fashion items. The end users of 80% of the goods reported to be dangerous and counterfeit were children; the products concerned included toys, childcare items and children's clothing.
- The most common reported danger (32%) was related to exposure to hazardous chemicals and toxins that could cause acute or long-term health issues from immediate or long-term exposure.
- Some 24% of the dangerous products recorded as counterfeit posed more than one danger to users.
- The causes of the risks identified included poorly constructed products, use of inferior supplies and components, and the lack of understanding of regulations or safety mechanisms.
- The analysis of the counterfeits uncovered 225 reported health and safety risks, led by chemical risk (32% of the total), followed by strangulation (17.3%), injuries (from mechanical dangers) (16.0%), electric shock (6.7%), damage to hearing (4.0%) and fire (4.0%).

A legislative proposal on a General Product Safety Regulation (GPSR) revising the GPSD was published in June 2021 and is being discussed in the European Parliament and Council. Stakeholders have been involved in the review process, with brand owner organisations proposing that the scope of the directive be expanded to include counterfeit unsafe products. The Commission pointed out that counterfeit products are already addressed in EU legislation, and unsafe products are in any case covered in the GPSD and in the proposed GPSR regardless of their authenticity. Even though counterfeit products can pose safety risks, it was noted, the safety of a given product has to be assessed and determined on the basis of a risk assessment. In this respect, the fundamental rule set out in the GPSD and GPSR proposal according to which all products placed on the EU market must be safe ensures that both authentic and counterfeit unsafe products are tackled.

Table 1.6 summarizes a list of products categories with the main risks identified.

Table 1.6. Counterfeit products with health and safety implications

Product (HS code)	Most frequent risk
Foodstuffs (02-21)	Microbiological, chemical
Pharmaceutical products (30)	Microbiological, chemical
Perfumery and cosmetics (33)	Chemical, microbiological
Soap (34)	Microbiological, chemical
Clothing, knitted or crotched (61)	Injuries, Strangulation, Chemical, Choking
Other made-up textile articles (63)	Injuries, Strangulation, Chemical, Choking
Jewellery (71)	Chemical
Electrical machinery and electronics (85)	Electric shock, Fire, Environment, Burns
Watches (91)	Chemical
Toys and games (95)	Chemical, choking, injuries, environment, damage to hearing, burns, strangulation
Vehicle parts (87)	Injuries, Fire

Overall the list contains a large number goods' categories. Even though, at the first glance some of them might seem counterintuitive, they pose serious health and safety threats to consumers.

For example, cases related to jewellery are reported to contain such toxic substances as heavy metals like lead and cadmium, as well as PVC and other plastics. This is aggravated by the fact that children can put jewellery in their mouths.

Other, somehow less intuitive examples, refer to health risks posed by watches and clothing. For watches, the main area of concern are dangerous chemicals and toxic heavy metals used for production of strap and watch case. For clothing, there are numerous instances of objects containing toxic materials, or made in a ways that poses risks of chocking or fire. For example, outfit for girls was described as posing: "a risk of strangulation and injuries for children because of the presence of drawstrings in the hood and waist area."

Another category are "other made-up textile articles". An example of a product from this category is a cushion cover that was made out of extremely toxic textile material containing dyes releasing the aromatic amine benzidine. When the product is in direct and prolonged contact with the skin, this aromatic amine may be absorbed by the skin causing cancer, cell mutations and affect reproduction.

2 Dangerous Products – Types of Risks

As indicated earlier, the overall, precise magnitude and scope of counterfeiting are unknown; assessments of the impact of substandard products on the health and safety of consumers thus relies heavily on anecdotal evidence. The anecdotal information, while imperfect, nevertheless provides useful insights into the serious risks that counterfeits can and have posed. The purpose of this section is to provide illustrations of the effects, across a broad range of products.

For analytical purposes, the damaging impacts of counterfeiting were classified into four areas: effects on (i) health, (ii) safety, (iii) environment and (iv) personal security.

Importantly, many dangerous products pose several risks at the same time. For example, a counterfeit pesticide can be harmful to the environment while at the same time posing health risks to people; fake spare parts (e.g. car battery) can pose safety and environmental risk; and a counterfeit medical device can pose both safety and health threats.

In addition, the presence of dangerous counterfeit products also damage the value of the brand and image of the producers of genuine products over time. For instance, those consumers who believed they were buying a genuine article when they in fact were buying a fake will be likely to blame the manufacturer of the genuine product if the fake did not fulfil expectations, thus creating a loss of goodwill. If consumers never discovered that they had been deceived they may be reluctant to buy another product from that manufacturer and may communicate the information to other potential buyers. Effects of this sort were reported to several surveys along the lines of "erosion of company name" or "destruction of brand reputation". Such indications came from respondents across numerous sectors including consumer electronics, information and computers, electrical equipment, food and drink, luxury goods, sportswear, automotive spare parts & car accessories and pharmaceuticals.

Effects on health

Counterfeit food, beverages, pharmaceuticals and related personal care items which have been improperly formulated or which contain ingredients that are harmful can have effects ranging from mild inconveniences to consumers, to life-threatening situations. Moreover, in the case of pharmaceuticals, the lack of active ingredients can deprive consumers of the possibility to treat diseases effectively, thus prolonging illnesses that would otherwise be treatable.

Pharmaceuticals

Substandard counterfeit medicines can affect individuals directly in a variety of ways, including: i) the adverse effects of incorrect active ingredients, ii) failure to cure or prevent future disease, thereby increasing mortality, morbidity and the prevalence of disease and iii) contributing to the progression of antimicrobial resistance and drug-resistant infections (WHO, 2017[9]). Moreover, the existence of ineffectual or dangerous counterfeits can contribute to a loss of confidence in health care professionals, health programmes and health systems, which can further undermine the well-being of persons.

WHO estimates indicate that between 72 000 and 169 000 children may die from pneumonia every year after receiving counterfeit drugs, and that fake anti-malarial medication might be responsible for an additional 116 000 deaths (WHO, 2017[9]). The effects on children can be alarming. One study of malaria-positive children in 39 sub-Saharan countries estimated that 120 000 children under five years of age died because of use of low-quality anti-malarials, including counterfeit and substandard products (Renschler et al., 2015[10]). Another study on the health consequences of falsified medicines analysed 48 incidents in which falsified medicines caused serious adverse effects to patients. These incidents involved approximately 7 200 casualties, including 3 604 deaths (Rahman, 2018[11]). The results of the study indicate that a similar number of incidents affect developing and developed countries alike, and the counterfeiters target all types of medications.

Forensic tests of suspect samples performed by the pharmaceutical industry demonstrate that counterfeit medicines could cause harm to patients in 90% of the cases tested. While many incidences of patient harm will likely go undetected, numerous examples have nevertheless emerged.[18] For example, a 2020 UK survey concludes that almost one-third (32%) of those who bought one or more counterfeit medicines experienced a health issue as a result.[19] There are numerous other documented cases in which patients have died or suffered harm due to an online purchase. In 2013, for example, people died after taking a counterfeit diet pill bought through an online drug seller.[20] The pill, sold as a weight loss aid through many illicit online pharmacies, contained BNP, which is also used in pesticides. Depending on the amount consumed, acute poisoning could occur with consumers. Reactions could include nausea, vomiting, restlessness, flushed skin, sweating, dizziness, headaches, rapid respiration and irregular heartbeat, possibly leading to coma and death.

Dangers have also surfaced with respect to counterfeit opioids, resulting in a safety alert being issued by the US Drug Enforcement Agency in September 2021.[21] The alert cites a sharp increase in the availability of counterfeit prescription pills containing fentanyl and methamphetamine. The counterfeit pills, mass-produced by criminal drug networks, were deceptively marketed as legitimate prescription pills, killing unsuspecting Americans at an unprecedented rate. More than 9.5 million pills had been seized at the time of the alert. Laboratory testing revealed a dramatic rise in the number of counterfeit pills containing at least two milligrams of fentanyl, which is considered a lethal dose.

The challenges related to illicit trade in pharmaceuticals became more significant with the COVID-19 pandemic, which provided criminals that run illicit trade networks with new opportunities for profits. Broken supply chains, strong demand for medicines, personal protective equipment and tests, combined with limited capacities of law enforcement officials to intercept the counterfeit products, contributed to a reshaping of the market for illicit products. Criminals clearly took advantage of the global pandemic, with enforcement authorities reporting a sharp increase in seizures of fake and substandard medicines, test kits and personal protective equipment (PPEs) as well as other medical products. In addition, recently, instances of counterfeit COVID-19 vaccines have been reported, posing a serious threat to the vaccination programmes.

Alcohol

Alcohol is an attractive market for illicit trade, which includes counterfeit and unbranded, bootlegged products, as well as products which are smuggled from countries where taxation is low, to countries where high taxes are imposed to discourage consumption. The high retail prices for legitimate alcohol, which reflects the high taxes imposed, have created incentives and opportunities for counterfeiters and other criminal organisations to both i) smuggle genuine products and ii) produce and market substandard products clandestinely. The illegally produced products are sometimes made with lower priced ingredients. This has raised serious health concerns as the rogue producers may use lower-priced methanol in their products in lieu of highly taxed ethanol (Box 2.1) (Lachenmeier Dirk W. Maria Neufeld and Jürgen Rehm, 2021[12]). It is estimated that methanol has a strong link to morbidity and mortality results in several thousand deaths per year worldwide. In addition to death, methanol consumption can have other serious effects, including a decreased level of consciousness, poor or no coordination, vomiting, abdominal pain, and/or could cause permanent blindness due to the destruction of the optic nerve.

> **Box 2.1. Examples of methanol poisoning**
>
> A methanol-poisoning outbreak occurred in the Czech Republic in 2012 from counterfeit alcohol and resulted in 140 people suffering health damage and more than 50 deaths. The mass poisoning in the Czech Republic was associated with a significant decrease of health-related quality of life for the survivors, as well as to long-term costs for the healthcare system.
>
> In Russia, 34 persons died from drinking illicit vodka containing methanol in October 2021, with another 25 hospitalized. Police investigation discovered a warehouse manufacturing plant in which over 600 litres of alcoholic spirits were seized, with a further 1,279 bottles of counterfeit alcohol discovered in the region affected by the contaminated alcohol during two days of widespread checks.
>
> *Sources*: (Lachenmeier Dirk W. Maria Neufeld and Jürgen Rehm, 2021[12]) and www.brusselstimes.com/news/188971/counterfeit-alcohol-in-russia-claims-34-lives/.

Other potentially toxic ingredients found in illicit alcohol include formic acid, which is contained in some antiseptic medicinal products that people drink instead of alcohol (i.e. surrogate products) (Lachenmeier, Neufeld and Rehm, 2021). Formic acid can lead to exacerbation of the chronic effects of ethanol by contributing to an excessive buildup of acid in the body (metabolic acidosis). Some of the toxicological studies from Kazakhstan, Russia, and Ukraine indicate that patients treated for acute poisonings with surrogate alcohol also showed traces of methanol, isopropanol, acetone, fusel alcohols, bio-solvents, and unknown and unidentified alcohols.

Other contaminants found in illicit alcohol include aflatoxins (i.e. toxins produced by certain fungi that are found on agricultural crops such as maize, peanuts, cottonseed, and tree nuts), hydrocyanic acid (a highly poisonous hydrogen cyanide product), cyanide derivatives (including ethyl carbamate), heavy metal contamination (with lead, arsenic, or cadmium), and elevated levels of acetaldehyde (which might contribute to the carcinogenicity of ethanol) (Lachenmeier Dirk W. Maria Neufeld and Jürgen Rehm, 2021[12]).

Importantly, during the COVID-19 pandemic, additional volumes of illegal (including counterfeit) alcohol have entered markets through vulnerable supply chains, weak enforcement, and porous borders. Closures of some businesses and disruptions in transport methods have led to significant distortions in supply chains. These distortions have been generating both: excess supplies of goods (for example, in cases of closures in the HoReCa sector that did not need contracted alcohol anymore) and unsatisfied demand (in cases of limited access to existing suppliers). In all these cases, criminals exploited these opportunities for illicit profits.

Cosmetics

Government and industry studies and testing have discovered that some of the ingredients that are used to produce counterfeit cosmetics and fragrances are dangerous. Such cosmetics often contain known carcinogens, such as arsenic, beryllium, and cadmium, along with high levels of aluminum and presence of microbiological contamination.[22] Some of these products have caused acne, psoriasis, rashes, and eye infections. Counterfeit fragrances have been found to contain DEHP, classified by the US Environmental Protection Agency as a probable human carcinogen. These counterfeit perfumes and colognes, which sometimes contain urine, have been known to cause serious skin rashes.

In 2020, the Los Angeles Police Department raided the city's Fashion District and seized USD 700,000 worth of counterfeit cosmetics. Tests revealed that the seized products, which included fake Anastasia, NARS, MAC, Urban Decay and Kylie Cosmetics, contained high levels of bacteria and animal waste (Holland, 2020[13]). In the United Kingdom, authorities uncovered hundreds of thousands of pounds worth of counterfeit beauty products in 2018.[23] Use of the products risked chemical burns and skin rashes. Moreover, exposure to the mercury in the cosmetics could have toxic effects on the nervous system, digestive and immune systems, lungs, kidneys, skin and eyes. Some of the counterfeit seized by the authorities were also found to have illegal levels of the skin-whitening agent hydroquinone.

Toothpaste

In 2019, the Ministry of Health in Costa Rica, issued an alert indicating that two types of counterfeit toothpaste of a known brand were being sold on the market. Tests on seized products confirmed that the product contained diethylene glycol (DEG), which was not declared on the labeling and that could be harmful to health. DEG is a compound that is used as an antifreeze and sometimes as a glycerin replacement thickener; the legitimate producer, Colgate-Palmolive, indicated that it did not use it in its toothpaste. It is rapidly absorbed through the digestive and respiratory tract and by prolonged skin contact. Its use in cosmetic products is prohibited in the country.[24]

Counterfeit toothpaste of a well-known brand was also detected on the US market, in 2007. The FDA issued two alerts in that year, both indicating the presence of DEG in toothpaste that it tested, which included products indicating South Africa and China as the countries of manufacture.[25] While the agency was not aware of any instances of poisonings from the toothpaste, it was concerned about potential risks from chronic exposure to DEG and exposure to DEG in certain populations, such as children and individuals with kidney or liver disease. DEG in toothpaste reportedly has a low but meaningful risk of toxicity and injury to these populations.

Contact lenses

A major online retailer of colored contact lenses in the United States pleaded guilty in 2016 to running an international operation importing counterfeit and misbranded contact lenses from suppliers in Asia and then selling them over the Internet without a prescription to tens of thousands of US customers.[26] Such lenses are medical devices that must receive FDA authorization to enter the United States. After purchasing the lenses, many customers complained directly about their quality and questioned whether the contact lenses were genuine and FDA approved. The retailer admitted that some of the contact lenses he sold were tested and found to be contaminated with potentially hazardous bacteria. The case revealed that the retailer received at least USD 1.2 million in gross revenue from the illegal enterprise, including approximately USD 200,000 alone from the sale of counterfeit Ciba Vision FreshLook COLORBLENDS.

Effects on safety

Clandestinely produced, substandard counterfeit products raise serious safety concerns for a wide range of consumer products. Insights into the magnitude and scope of the problem can be obtained through the experience of Underwriters Laboratories (UL), which is an independent worldwide body that tests and certifies the safety of products. Once certified, tested products are entitled to bear a "UL" mark, which can be important for enhancing consumer confidence in the safety of the products concerned. This could be particularly important for lesser-known brands that have not established a reputation. The UL mark thus has considerable value, and counterfeiters have used it fraudulently to deceive consumers. In 2019, the company worked successfully with partners to remove 3.8 million counterfeit UL marked products from the market (UL, 2020[14]).

UL activities have also included efforts to disrupt fraudulent online trade. In 2019, UL's Brand Protection team monitored websites for listings containing potentially dangerous products bearing counterfeit or unauthorized UL marks (UL, 2020[14]). Their efforts resulted in the removal of more than 86,873 listings in 25 economies,[27] up from 8,370 on 2018. In 2020, UL launched an initiative to crack down on deceptive practices to combat fraudulent personal protective equipment (PPE). The organization's brand protection team initially reviewed over 40,000 online supplier listings, preventing over 300 million deceptive products from entering the marketplace.[28]

Table 2.1 lists products that have been found in recent months by UL to bear a counterfeit (unauthorized) UL mark. The testing body recommends that many of the products be removed from service and/or be taken off the market in light of the potential safety risks, including fire and electric shock.

Table 2.1. Examples of unauthorized use of UL mark during 2020-22

Product	Date of notice	Note
Certain SAFT lithium/thionyl chloride batteries	01-2022	Batteries concerned are counterfeit. Unknown if any safety requirements met. UL recommends removal from market.
Certain ADVENTECH motors	10-2021	Unknown if any safety requirements met. UL recommends that product not be used.
Certain KARTAR fire sprinklers	09-2021	Unknown if any safety requirements met. UL recommends that product be removed from service.
Certain Ningbo Xuanhua extension cords	09-2021	Cords do not comply with safety standards. UL recommends that the product not be used.
Certain ABBOTECH wall outlets	08-2021	Outlets do not comply with safety standards. UL recommends that the product not be installed.
Hunan Aomeng electrical cords and appliance wiring material	06-2021	UL mark has not been authorized for these products. UL requests that it be contacted if products found on market.
Certain Love Attitude cleansing products	06-2021	Unknown of the products comply with any UL sustainability standards. UL recommends that products not be used.
Proextinseg fire extinguishers	04-2021	Extinguishers are counterfeit. Unknown if any safety requirements met. UL recommends that product not be used.
Certain Clariitonix communication cable	03-2021	Cable does not comply with safety standards. UL recommends that the cable not be used and be removed form service,
Certain LEMSIR portable energy-stored power packs	01-2021	Unknown if any safety requirements met. UL recommends that the products concerned not be used.
Certain eLink USB chargers	11-2020	Unknown if any safety requirements met. UL recommends that the products concerned not be used.
Certain pressure restricting valves from an unknown manufacturer	09-2020	Unknown if any safety requirements met. UL recommends that the products concerned be replaced.
Certain UNIIMAX e-scooters	07-2020	Unknown if any safety requirements met. UL recommends that products not be used.
Certain Songling cordless massagers	07-2020	Unknown if any safety requirements met. UL recommends that products not be used.
Certain Yeiser lead acid batteries	04-2020	Unknown if any safety requirements met. UL recommends that products not be used.

Source: (UL, n.d.[15]).

Following are specific examples of a range of counterfeit products that raised safety concerns in recent years.

Toys and children's equipment

Counterfeit versions of popular toys are an ongoing problem, which is exacerbated during holiday periods when genuine products are often in short supply. The availability of lower priced alternatives on the Internet further complicates the situation, as buyers may be attracted to the lower prices, not knowing that the product they are buying is a fake, and could well be substandard and unsafe for children. L.O.L. dolls, for example, are highly popular toys which have been counterfeited with substandard products that contain phthalates, a chemical which can damage the liver, kidneys, lungs and reproductive system.[29]

In December 2018, a four-year-old boy broke fake Magformers magnetic building blocks and swallowed several loose magnets (Kent, 2020[16]). As the ingested magnets tried to connect to each other, they caused significant intestinal damage, resulting in hospitalization and surgery to repair and remove his damaged intestine. Genuine Magformers toys are subjected to regular safety testing to ensure the small magnets are encapsulated safely and will not come loose during play. This was not the case with the non-compliant product.

Magnets already have been flagged as an area of concern when used in toys in general (Frankel, 2019[17]). Rare-earth magnets are particularly dangerous because they can be 10 times stronger than the ordinary magnets. As mentioned above, multiple, small rare-earth magnets are swallowed, they can pull together inside the intestines, potentially causing life-threatening holes and blockages. Their use by counterfeiters, who are not likely to take adequate precautions, is therefore a major concern.

Counterfeit baby strollers have also raised safety concerns. In 2019, online advertisements for "4 in 1 Baby car seat and Stroller" falsely linked the product to a popular brand called Doona.[30] The counterfeit, listed for USD 299, which was USD 200 cheaper than a genuine Doona. The counterfeit product broke into pieces and failed to meet even the most basic of safety standards set by US regulators in a 30 mile per hour crash test. The test indicated that a child could be put in grave danger, with potential injuries to the child's chest, neck or head, which could result in a traumatic brain injury. The dummy used in the test fractured and slid forward along with plastic pieces that had broken off the car seat. In an identical crash test, the genuine Doona product met crash requirements and remained in one piece.

Recreational equipment

Hoverboards were a popular gift item in 2015. Many consumers, however, discovered that their hoverboards overheated, putting themselves and their homes at risk.[31] In response, the US Consumer Product Safety Commission declared many hoverboards unsafe and recommended only the sale of hoverboards that met UL's requirements (Box 2.2). This posed a challenge to many distributors holding large inventories of items that did not meet the requirements. In response, some elected to put a counterfeit UL mark on the items. In one instance, UL located an online business that was misusing the UL mark, resulting in the seizure of more than 4,800 counterfeit products.

> **Box 2.2. CPSC safety alert on hoverboards, 2017**
>
> "Since fall 2015, CPSC has led the way in warning the public about the dangers posed by hoverboards. CPSC is aware of more than 250 self-balancing scooter/hoverboard incidents related to fires or overheating. In March 2017, a 2-year-old girl and a 10-year-old girl died in a house fire ignited by a hoverboard in Harrisburg, Pennsylvania. In addition, CPSC has reports of 13 burn injuries, three smoke inhalation injuries and more than USD 4 million in property damage related to hoverboards."
>
> CPSC recommended that consumers take a number of steps to reduce the risk of fire, including purchasing only those items which were compliant with UL safety standards. The agency cautioned that hoverboards should never be purchased from a kiosk, a second-hand seller, or an online retailer without proof that the item was compliant with these standards.
>
> *Source*: (CPSC, n.d.[18]).

Electrical and electronic equipment

Many types of electrical and electronic equipment have been counterfeited, some, like semiconductors, are used in a broad range of products that demand high performance, which is something that cheaply manufactured articles cannot achieve. Their incorporation into other products complicate their detection, with potentially serious consequences.

Semiconductors

The Covid pandemic disrupted supply chains and resulted in shortages in many products, including semiconductors.[32] In response to shortages, hard-pressed suppliers and businesses explored new ways to meet their demand for the semiconductors, reaching beyond their traditional sources to meet demand. Increased sourcing of parts through non-traditional channels, such as the Internet, created new forms of risk as the situation provided opportunities for counterfeiters to infiltrate markets.

The risk that counterfeits pose to product safety are significant. While semiconductor companies invest heavily in developing, manufacturing, testing and supporting products that will operate at a high level and reliably, counterfeits are often "harvested" from electronic waste using crude and poorly-controlled processes that result in counterfeit semiconductors having far higher failure rates than genuine semiconductors.[33] Some counterfeit semiconductors will reportedly fail immediately when electrically tested or first used, while others may fail shortly thereafter. The use of counterfeits has already been linked to a number of potentially life-threatening incidents, including:[34]

- *Medical devices*: A counterfeit semiconductor component was identified in an automated external defibrillator, resulting in a defibrillator over-voltage condition. Failure to detect and address this issue could have resulted in improper electrical shocks being applied to heart attack victims, thus jeopardizing their lives.
- *Household appliances*: A counterfeit semiconductor component caused a fire in the control circuitry in a vacuum cleaner for residential use. This fire was successfully contained, but it had the potential to result in major property damage or even loss of life.
- *Air travel*: A counterfeit semiconductor failed in a power supply used for airport landing lights. This did not result in any reported airline take-off or landing incidents, but the potential for such incidents was apparent.

Batteries

Lithium-ion batteries are becoming increasingly common, as their use in devices such as smartphones and tablets rise, along with increased use in power tools, lawn mowers and other yard devices, as well as toys (Box 2.3).[35] The batteries, however, pose safety hazards that require the attention of consumers generally. The risk of harm, however, is magnified when the batteries are not manufactured and tested to ensure adherence to standards. Consumers thus need to be wary about purchasing unbranded batteries which may not have been thoroughly tested by independent testing bodies, but they must also be careful in purchasing certified, branded batteries as these batteries have been and continue to be counterfeited.

> **Box 2.3. Lithium battery safety concerns**
>
> Lithium cells and batteries power countless items that support everyday life from portable computers, cordless tools, mobile telephones, watches, to wheelchairs and motor vehicles. Our society has come to depend on lithium cells and batteries for an increasingly mobile lifestyle. Today's lithium cells and batteries are more energy dense than ever, bringing a steadily growing number of higher-powered devices to market.
>
> The risks posed by lithium cells and batteries are generally a function of type, size, and chemistry. Lithium cells and batteries can present both chemical (e.g. corrosive or flammable electrolytes) and electrical hazards. Unlike standard alkaline batteries, most lithium batteries manufactured today contain a flammable electrolyte and have an incredibly high energy density. They can overheat and ignite under certain conditions, such as a short circuit or improper design or assembly. Once ignited, lithium cell and battery fires can be difficult to extinguish. Additional, although infrequent, events can result in lithium cells and batteries experiencing thermal runaway, a chain reaction leading to a violent release of stored energy and flammable gas. This thermal runaway can propagate to other batteries or conductive materials nearby, potentially resulting in large scale thermal events with severe consequences.
>
> *Source*: PHMSA, 2021.

With respect to the nature of battery safety risks, counterfeit products may in particular be prone to failure and cause fires and explosions. They are typically produced by illegal enterprises, by manufacturers which typically lack the technical knowledge and understanding that are required for quality control, safety and shipping. Certifications are often falsified along with misleading performance claims, thereby compromising the safety of the lithium-ion products and eventually the devices that they are used in. High-quality components and safety mechanisms are needed in lithium-ion products for protection against off-nominal conditions.[36] Overcharging, over discharging, extreme temperatures, and external or internal shorts are some of the off-nominal conditions that products may experience in use which may result in thermal runaway and fire.

Substandard counterfeit batteries may also affect the performance of the devices that they are used to power. Low quality products which have not been subject to rigorous controls are likely to affect the overall performance and safety of battery powered devices and appliances, affecting the uniformity of the cells inside a battery pack thereby making the battery management system complex or inoperable or in some cases the components that are used in the battery management system (BMS) may not be compatible with the charger or the application.

Lithium-ion products are considered dangerous goods and must be labeled as such when transported. Strict guidelines and restrictions must be followed and must meet UN test standards when being transported by air. Counterfeiters, however, may mislabel their products and not declare them as dangerous goods in order to avoid restrictions. Dropping such batteries during transportation may cause cells to undergo venting, thermal runaway, and fire. Incidents of fatal crashes and fires in airplanes have in fact been linked to cargoes containing undeclared lithium-ion products.

To help lower the risk of adverse events, the International Air Transport Association (IATA) has developed comprehensive risk assessment guidance for the aviation industry which provides concrete steps for evaluating the dangers inherent in transporting the batteries (IATA, 2021[19]). The guidance makes specific reference to the availability of lithium batteries which do not meet UN safety standards (which may be counterfeit or simply substandard), in some parts of the world, and on the Internet. Such batteries pose an increased risk that they may fail or catch fire when subjected to the shocks and loadings encountered under the normal conditions of transport.

The guidance further notes that safety concerns are not restricted to baggage and cargo. While lithium batteries, whether shipped on their own or packed with equipment, are not permitted in airmail, numerous websites advertise the batteries for sale with delivery by airmail as an option. According to IATA, there have, in fact, been a number of incidents involving lithium batteries in airmail.

Power adapters

An adapter is a device that converts power from an electrical outlet into a form that an electronic device can use (i.e. commonly from 100-240 volts, to 5 volts). Many brands of adapters are available from retailers and many brands are also available for purchasing on the Internet, at prices ranging from less than USD 2 for a simple charger available online, to more than USD 30 dollars for more sophisticated products. The design of the adapters and the materials used in their construction are critical to their operating properly and safely (UL, 2020a). Leading manufacturers and companies devote significant resources and money to make their adapters safe and subject their adapters to rigorous testing for safety and reliability.

Substandard adapters have been shown to be potentially highly dangerous. In 2013, a man from Thailand was found dead holding his Apple iPhone which was plugged into a wall outlet (UL, 2020[20]). An investigation conducted by the government determined that the Apple adapter was in fact counterfeit and was improperly shielded or grounded. In 2014, it is believed that a phone charger that had not been certified to applicable safety standards sent a high-voltage electrical pulse into an Australian woman's phone, which transferred to the earphones she had connected to a laptop, resulting in her being electrocuted.[37]

The scope of the problem is alarming. In 2020, UL posted a white paper containing the results of an investigation in which it tested 400 counterfeit Apple adapters to assess their safety (UL, 2020[20]). The adapters bearing counterfeit UL certification marks were obtained from multiple sources in eight different countries around the world, including the United States, Canada, Colombia, China, Thailand and Australia. An electric strength test was carried out on the adapters to determine how well they were isolated from the electrical mains. If the amount of current flowing was above a specified threshold, the unit was found to have insufficient isolation and was judged as unsafe, with a significant potential for electric shock. The adapters were also subject to a touch current test, which serves to measure the amount of current that could potentially flow through a person's body when that person comes into contact with the product. If too much current leaks through, the unit is said to have insufficient isolation and is considered to be unsafe, with a risk of electrocuting the user.

Twenty-two adapters were immediately damaged during the process of energizing or during the leakage current test, with 12 samples having a very high leakage current, which was high enough to result in electrocution. With regard to the electric strength test, only three of the four hundred samples passed, which translates into a 99 percent failure rate. Construction reviews found problems with the isolation transformer design in selected devices. The internal components were vastly different from those used in genuine UL Listed Apple adapters. Post-testing analysis also revealed a complete lack of triple isolation wire used for the secondary windings; neither the primary nor secondary windings were separated properly, which was the major reason for the high failure rate on the electric strength test.

Automotive parts

The global automotive aftermarket for replacement parts and accessories is large, accounting to more than USD 390 billion in 2020, according to one research organization.[38] The size of the market, and the increasing role of the Internet in the market have made it an attractive market for counterfeiters. Counterfeit products pose potentially serious risks to consumers as they are not made to the specifications of the original manufacturer, are not subject to quality control tests, and often fail to perform as intended, which could result in catastrophic failures with potentially fatal consequences.[39] US Customs seizure statistics reveal that counterfeit safety components like brake pads, air bags, wheels, and suspension parts are commonplace. Additional counterfeit parts reported to have been seized by law enforcement include seat belts, oil and air filters, windshields, microchips, and spark plugs.

The Automotive Anti-Counterfeiting Council (A2C2) is actively engaged in combatting counterfeits. The Council has identified a number of safety risks associated with substandard counterfeits, including:[40]

- Airbags: Many counterfeit airbags have been found to improperly deploy, or not deploy at all, posing a risk to vehicle occupants.
- Body and structural parts: Counterfeit vehicle hoods designed without crumple zones may penetrate the passenger compartment in a crash, putting vehicle occupants at greater risk.
- Brakes: Counterfeit brake pads have been found to be made of grass clippings and saw dust, which would likely jeopardize stopping ability. A test conducted by Mercedes-Benz revealed that counterfeit brake pads on cars driving at 100km/h on a dry surface took 25 metres longer to come to a complete halt.[41] In another BMW test, counterfeit brake pads started to smoke and disintegrate early on in standard testing procedures.
- Engine and drive train: Counterfeit spark plugs can overheat and may lead to fire. Counterfeit oil filters can cause sudden engine failure.
- Suspension parts: Counterfeit suspension parts made of substandard materials have shown higher rates of failure, which may place drivers and passengers at risk.
- Wheels and tires: Counterfeit wheels have exhibited compromised structural integrity by cracking after hitting a pothole at just over 30 miles per hour. Counterfeit tires often fail on air pressure and feature cracking, bulging, blistering, rippling in the sidewall or abnormal treadwear patterns.[42]

Particular attention has been paid in recent years to the proliferation of counterfeit parts available on online ecommerce platforms. In October 2021, the organization urged one major platform to ban the sale of all airbags on its site, noting that counterfeit airbags are typically comprised completely of counterfeit components, but that such airbags have also been found to be comprised of certain used original equipment manufacturer (OEM) components cobbled together with counterfeit components so as to appear to be complete OEM airbags.39 The fake airbags are reportedly difficult to spot, often appearing nearly identical to genuine, original equipment parts; they can, however, be unsafe and result in catastrophic failures, with fatal consequences.

Personal protective equipment

The Covid pandemic resulted in a sharp rise in demand for personal protective equipment, by medical professionals and the general public alike. The market was flooded by products, some of which falsely attached trademarked certification to deceive consumers on the efficacy of the products. One of the products which was widely counterfeited was respirators.

In the United States, the National Institute for Occupational Safety and Health (NIOSH), which is a part of the Centers for Disease Control and Prevention (CDC) oversees the National Personal Protective Technology Laboratory, which evaluates and approves respirators which meet government standards. In the case of N95 respirators, it ensures that the products in question filters 95% of airborne articles.[43] The use of the NIOSH label obligates the applicant to whom it was issued to maintain the quality level of manufactured respirators and assure that the respiratory protection device (RPD) is manufactured to the drawings and specifications upon which the certificate of approval is based.

The approval labels contain important information to assist users in understanding the respirator, its protections, cautions and limitations, and approved configuration of components. According to NIOSH, use of components not listed on the full NIOSH approval label constitutes configurations not included in the approval and could cause serious injury and/or death to the user (Metzler, 2011[21]) When the agency discovers counterfeits, it alerts the public through public notices which are posted on the Internet. In 2020, some 21 notices of counterfeit products were posted, up from 16 in 2019; in 2021, the number slipped to 13.[44]

Respirators similar to the N95 have been designed and tested to meet international standards.[45] The most widely available are KN95 respirators, which are a Chinese version. Other examples include 1st, DL2, DL3, DS2, DS3, FFP2, FFP3, KN100, KP95, KP100, P2, P3, PFF2, PFF3, R95, and Special. NIOSH evaluated KN95 masks in 2020 and 2021, finding that about 60% of those tested did not meet their intended requirements.

Environmental impact

Substandard counterfeit products can have environmentally damaging consequences. Both the manufacture and the disposal of counterfeit items can have major impacts on the environment. In the manufacture of products, the use of toxic dyes, unlawful disposal of chemicals, and unregulated air pollution are problematic (UNODC, ≥2013). With respect to the disposal of counterfeit goods, the WTO Agreement on Trade-Related Aspects of Intellectual Property Rights (TRIPS Agreement) requires the WTO members to provide in their domestic legal framework for the remedy of destroying or disposing of IP infringing goods; the practical implementation of this, however, is daunting (WIPO, 2017[22])

Firstly, the large volume and wide diversity of IP infringing goods make managing seizure operations, from the processing of items to their destruction, a difficult undertaking for enforcement agencies (Guard, 2017). While the costs of the operations should ideally be recovered from the infringers or criminal organizations that produced or imported the illicit goods, in practice the costs are most often incurred by right holders and taxpayers. The logistics of storing, destroying or disposing of products, or recycling them in an environmentally safe way with minimal health and safety implications, is in itself often a daunting task, especially when hazardous materials are involved. This is particularly difficult in countries where technical capacity, appropriate storage and waste facilities, regulatory control and funds are more limited. In countries with more robust regulatory frameworks, specialized facilities for environmentally safe waste disposal and recycling of seized IP infringing goods can diminish the scope of environmental damage. The task for all, however, can be further complicated following coordinated customs seizure operations in which a large number of IP infringing goods are confiscated over a short timeframe, creating a volume of IP infringing products that may stretch the enforcement authorities' ability to effectively and correctly store and dispose of them. In addition to limited storage capacity, extended litigation procedures or the protracted time required for analysing seized goods to determine their composition or hazard before destruction or disposal can further complicate the situation.

The techniques for disposing of IP infringing goods include incineration, open burning, recycling, shredding, crushing, chemical treatment, encapsulation, inertization and landfill (WIPO, 2017[22]). A survey carried out by React, a non-profit organization engaged in combatting counterfeit trade, indicates that most of the billions of counterfeit items seized are in fact incinerated. Open burning is by far the most harmful disposal method, with the potential of devastating and long-term effects on both the environment and human health (WIPO, 2017[22]). Despite this, it is frequently used and is the main method employed at showcase events aimed at raising public awareness of the counterfeit problem. Burning products with their plastic packaging materials, which is often the case, can release a large volume of toxic fumes such as persistent organic pollutants (POPs), which are resistant to environmental degradation and affect both workers and waste pickers with direct exposure to the toxic fumes, while raising the potential for polluting soils and waterways. Toxins can be absorbed by people through smoke, fumes and vapors, or following settlement on the surrounding environment through bioaccumulation or bio-magnification in the food chain. Moreover, exposure to smoke and vapors can cause respiratory ailments, headaches and eye problems while emissions of POPs and other toxins are linked to i) certain types of cancers, ii) liver problems, iii) impairment of the immune system, the endocrine system and reproductive functions and iv) effects on the developing nervous system and other developmental events.

The disposal of products in non-sanitary and open landfills can also result in environmental and potential health impacts through the escape of contaminating or toxic leachate, which can pollute soils, groundwater and inland/coastal waterways, while releasing foul odors and spawning disease vectors (WIPO, 2017[22]). In addition, such landfills usually attract waste pickers, which can expose those individuals to harmful materials directly or through toxic releases when scavenged materials such as e-wastes (i.e. discarded electrical or electronic devices) are burned for copper and other metals.

Countries have handled the destruction of counterfeits in various ways, with far-reaching implications for the environment. Panelists in a 2021 UL virtual symposium recounted an instance where a pile of goods in a developing country containing toys, electronic goods and textiles was doused with gasoline in an open field, without due regard to the environmental consequences. In other instances, counterfeit goods were reportedly simply buried in the sand or in forests (UL, 2021[23]). On the other hand, in the United States, the government contracts with organizations that store and oversee the destruction of most counterfeit merchandise. The merchandise is typically incinerated, though there are exceptions for some products, such as tires, where shredding and recycling is preferred in light of the serious adverse environmental effects of tire burning. The potential to move counterfeits from jurisdictions which have limited capacity to destroy goods to ones which are in better position to do so has appeal, but legal constraints limit, if not prohibit, such traffic.

Pesticides and agrochemicals

Substantial quantities of counterfeit pesticides and agrochemicals are traded internationally. They are sold untested and unauthorized and are generally toxic, containing components very different from the original product (WIPO, 2017[22]) Moreover, they can have far lower flashpoints (which creates a transport risk) and may also contain illegal or banned POPs. With respect to transport, inadequate containers can provide an extra hazard for both storage and transport of these goods.

Use of counterfeit pesticides can have devastating effects on unsuspecting users (UL, 2021[23]) . In some areas, use of counterfeit products has destroyed crops and poisoned the fields for subsequent years, with severe economic and health consequences for the farming villages concerned. Moreover, substandard pesticides that are not strong enough to kill insects could result in the creation of more robust species of superbugs that could further damage farming. Consideration also needs to be given to the possibility of risky transportation by counterfeiters. Improperly shipped merchandise that ends up in waterways would have a pronounced effect on ecosystems.

Disposal of organic pesticides in an environmentally safe way (except those containing metals or arsenic), requires incineration at temperatures exceeding 1100° C. The risk of dioxin and furan formation can be reduced by an incinerator design; however, both the ash and filters may contain some toxic elements that require careful treatment and disposal.

Pharmaceuticals, cosmetics and medical equipment

The best environmental option for the disposal of most counterfeit pharmaceuticals is high temperature incineration with appropriate gas flue treatment to capture toxic gases is the most effective option for the disposal of counterfeit pharmaceuticals (WIPO, 2017[22]). The most widely practiced method for the disposal in developing countries is, however, non-sanitary open landfills, which is not environmentally friendly and should only be considered if pharmaceuticals can be immobilized through encapsulation, which is an inexpensive treatment that involves the filling of containers with solid or semi-solid pharmaceuticals to 75 per cent of their capacity, or inertization, which involves the prior removal of all pharmaceuticals from their packaging, the crushing of the counterfeit medicines using a grinder or road roller and the mixing of this material with other ingredients to form a homogenous solid which can be disposed of in landfill.

Information and communication technology and other electronic devices

Counterfeit electronic products contain many of the same materials as genuine electronic goods, including hazardous toxic substances such as lead, mercury, cadmium, arsenic, beryllium and brominated flame retardants, but also gold, silver, copper, palladium, cobalt, aluminum, lithium and rare earth metals (WIPO, 2017[22]). The most environmentally safe and beneficial form of disposal is through the recycling, with the recovery of the valuable metals offering significant financial dividends. While developed countries have licensed recycling facilities in which salvageable materials can be safely extracted, recycling of e-waste in developing countries is frequently conducted through informal recycling practices that are unregulated, usually informal and sometimes illegal and practiced by people with little personal protection equipment or technological support and a lack of awareness of the potential health risks. This can pose serious consequences for both public health and the environment.

In informal recycling, plastics are often openly burned at low temperatures either as a method of disposal or to salvage metals from the electronic products (WIPO, 2017[22]). This can release heavy metals into the environment as well as toxic emissions and residues, often carcinogenic, from the plastics. Moreover, the de-soldering of circuit boards likewise results in the release of highly toxic lead saturated fumes while the use of solvents, reagents and acids to remove precious metals in open acid baths can have adverse health and environmental impacts. Furthermore, most of these processes are highly inefficient so that only a fraction of the potential recoverable valuable metals is actually extracted.

Personal security

The growing role and impact of the Internet and, more generally, information and communication technology have been of great interest to cyber criminals, who have hacked their way to new markets, defrauding a growing population of consumers. One of the techniques that they have used is through the sale of adulterated counterfeit software that is designed to access and misuse the personal information of users, with potentially devastating consequences to their personal finances, privacy and security.

A survey published by the BSA and the Software Alliance in 2016 found that some 39 percent of all software installed on computers was not properly licensed (BSA, 2016[24]). The study found further that there was a strong correlation between malware and unlicensed software. Microsoft notes that each year tens of thousands of people report to Microsoft that they bought software that they later learned was counterfeit.[46] In many cases, the firm reports, illegitimate software downloads may be riddled with malware, including computer viruses, Trojan horses, spyware, or botware, designed to damage a computer, destroy data, compromise security, or steal one's identity (Box 2.4).

> **Box 2.4. Street sales of counterfeit Microsoft software**
>
> Several years ago, Microsoft caried out a market test in which counterfeit Windows and Office software was purchased from four different sellers in local markets, in Melbourne. The disks were then tested
>
> - Five out of the six Microsoft Office disks were infected with malware while six out of the twelve Windows disks could not be installed and run. Of the other six disks which could be run and tested successfully, the following was observed:
>   - Two were infected with malware;
>   - All the six copies had Windows Update disabled;
>   - All the six copies had the Windows Firewall rules changed.
> - Of the total of twelve counterfeit software copies that could be installed successfully (six Office and six Windows) and tested, the following was affirmed:
>   - Seven copies (58%) were infected with malware;
>   - A total of 20 instances of six different types of malware code were found.
>
> *Source*: www.thewindowsclub.com/consequences-risks-pirated-counterfeit-software.

The impact of adulterated counterfeit software was also examined in a 2013 study by IDC (IDC, 2013[25]) It found that:

- One third of PC software in the world is counterfeit. Because of the link between counterfeit software and IT security issues from malware, this posed a danger for consumers and businesses alike.
- In lab tests that included 533 tests of Web sites and P2P networks offering counterfeit software and counterfeit CDs/DVDs, IDC encountered tracking cookies/spyware 78% of the time when downloading software from the Internet and Trojans and other malicious adware 36% of the time. On the CDs/DVDs that were actually installable, Trojans and malicious adware were found in 20% of the time.

Once detected, consumers and enterprises had to invest considerable time and money to identify the corrupted software, repair their systems, recover lost data, and dealing with identity theft. In the case of consumers, the cost per incident was estimated to average from USD 60 on the Asia Pacific area, to USD 203 in North America. In total, consumers were estimated to have spent 1.5 billion hours and USD 22 billion to address the problems caused by the counterfeit software.

The costs, however, varied considerably even within regions. In the United States, professional services for restoring corrupted data files on home PCs were estimated to be as much as USD 2,500. Moreover, some US households experienced personal losses of greater than USD 13,000, while having to spend as much as 500 hours over a period of years to clear up problems.

3 Trade in Potential Dangerous Counterfeit Products – Quantitative Analysis

This chapter presents the quantitative analysis of types of counterfeit goods with high probability of posing elevated health, safety and environmental risks. As discussed in Chapter 2, establishing the scope of counterfeits that such risks can take several approaches:

- A broad approach that looks at all products that on top of the general product safety obligation, need to meet specific safety standards, before entering the market.
- A focused approach that takes into account products categories that tend to dominate lists of safety alerts related with specific health, safety or environmental harms.

The broad scope

The domain of products captured by this approach is established by examining a sample of governance efforts aimed at providing quality norms and standards to products that are present on local markets. As discussed in Chapter 2, these include (i) the product specific safety norms in the European Union, (ii) the scope of the US Food and Drug Administration and (iii) discussion in the United States surrounding the SHOP SAFE Act.

Counterfeit products that have been seized in the product categories defined using the broad scope approach are then analysed, using the OECD/EUIPO database of global customs seizures of counterfeit goods. The product categories analyzed include:

- Foodstuffs (02-21)
- Beverages (22)
- Tobacco (24)
- Salt; sulphur; earths and stone; lime and cement (25)
- Pharmaceutical products (30)
- Fertilisers (31)
- Tanning or dyeing extracts (32)
- Perfumery and cosmetics (33)
- Soap; albuminoidal substances; glues; explosives (34-37)
- Miscellaneous chemical products (38)
- Plastic and articles thereof (39)
- Rubber and article thereof (40)
- Articles of leather; handbags (42)

- Wood and articles thereof (44)
- Printed articles (49)
- Silk; wool; and other vegetable textile fibres (50-53)
- Man-made filaments and staple fibres (54/55)
- Carpets and rugs (57)
- Other textiles not elsewhere classified (n.e.c). (59)
- Clothing, knitted or crocheted (61)
- Clothing and accessories, not knitted or crocheted (62/65)
- Other made-up textile articles (63)
- Footwear (64)
- Articles of stone, plaster and cement (68)
- Ceramic products (69)
- Glass and glassware (70)
- Jewellery (71)
- Iron and steel; and articles thereof (72/73)
- Copper; nickel; aluminium; lead; zinc; tin; and articles thereof (74-81)
- Tools and cutlery of base metal (82)
- Miscellaneous articles of base metal (83)
- Machinery and mechanical appliances (84)
- Electrical machinery and electronics (85)
- Railway (86)
- Vehicles' parts (87)
- Aircraft (88)
- Ships (89)
- Optical; photographic; medical apparatus (90)
- Watches (91)
- Furnitures (94)
- Toys and games (95)
- Miscellaneous manufactured articles (66/67/96)

Seizure data indicate that there were over 400,000 seizures of products in potentially dangerous product categories worldwide between 2017 and 2019. The dangerous fakes seized were destined to almost 150 economies and originated from more than 190 different countries. The analysis of this broad scope is followed by the analysis of a more focused scope.

Products impacted

The scope of dangerous goods' categories that are subject to infringement is broad. However, the intensity of counterfeiting and piracy differs significantly from one product category to another. This is illustrated in Figure 3.1 below, which indicates that between 2017 and 2019, interceptions were concentrated in a relatively limited number of HS chapters.

From 2017 to 2019, the highest number of seizures among the dangerous fakes intercepted corresponded to ready to wear items (footwear, clothing), luxury goods (leather goods, watches) and electronic appliances. Other items included spare parts, optical and medical apparatus as well as pharmaceuticals.

Figure 3.1. Main product categories of dangerous goods subject to counterfeiting, 2017-19

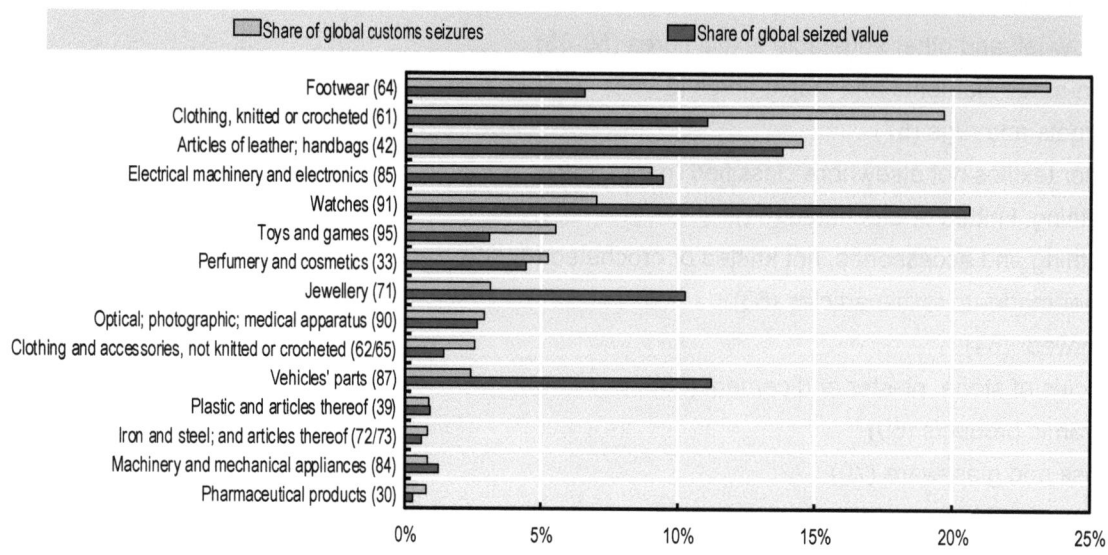

Source: OECD/EUIPO database.

Trade routes

From 2017 to 2019, the dangerous fakes seized mostly came from Asian countries, with eight of these countries accounting for around 84% of global seizures of dangerous fakes. As shown by Figure 3.2, these Asian countries were led by China (52%) and Hong Kong (China) (27%). They were followed by Turkey, which was the provenance economy for 8% of global seizures of dangerous fakes.

Figure 3.2. Main provenance economies of dangerous fakes, 2017-19

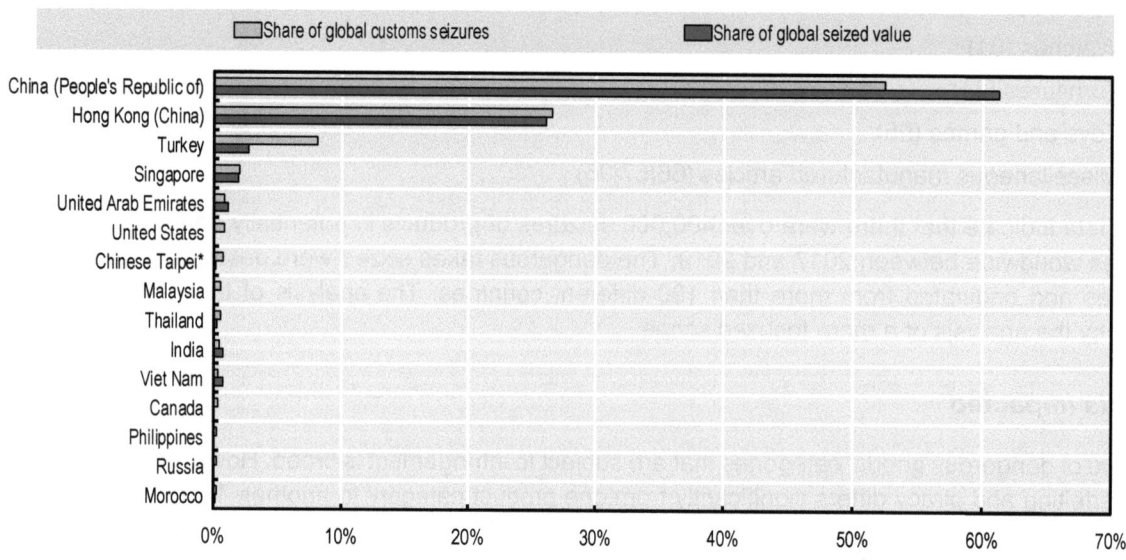

Source: OECD/EUIPO database.

The United Sates and the European Union countries were the main destination economies of counterfeit dangerous goods during 2017-19. Figure 3.3 indicates that 37% of global seizures of dangerous goods were destined to the United States. The European countries most targeted by counterfeiting of dangerous fakes were Germany (21%), Belgium (9%), Italy (6%) and Denmark (3%).

Figure 3.3. Main destination economies of dangerous fakes, 2017-19

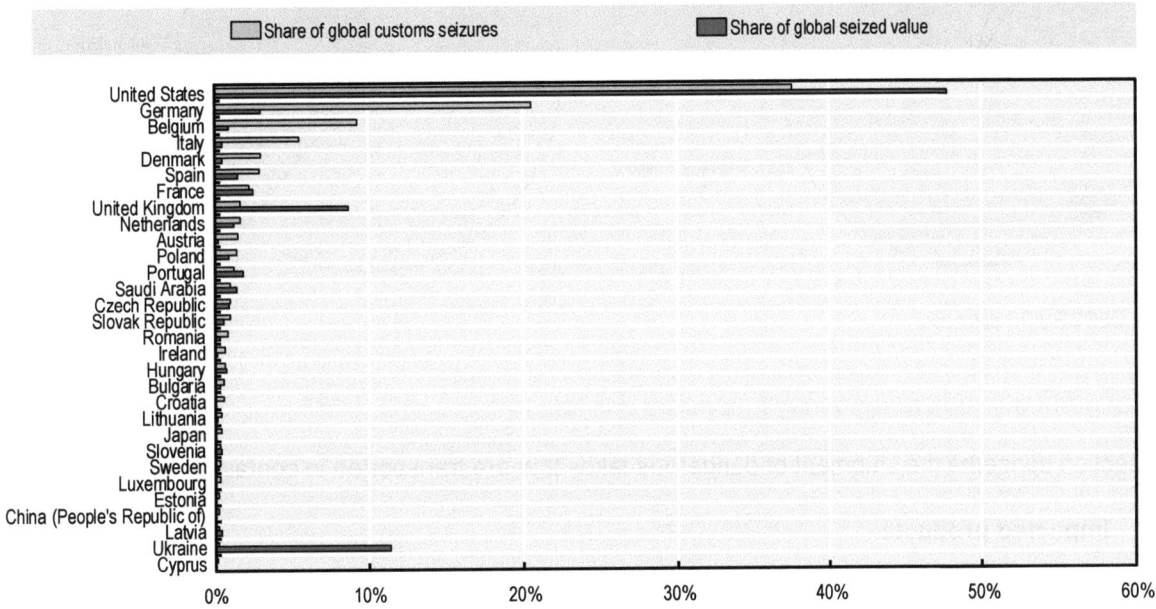

Source: OECD/EUIPO database.

Transport methods

As shown by Figure 3.4, the postal service (59% of global customs seizures of dangerous fakes) was the preferred conveyance method for shipping the dangerous goods between 2017 and 2019. It was followed by air and express courier, which represented 16% of global customs seizures of dangerous goods.

In terms of global seized value, shipments by sea was prominent. They represented more than 60% of the global seized value of dangerous fakes.

Figure 3.4. Conveyance methods of dangerous goods subject to counterfeiting, 2017-19

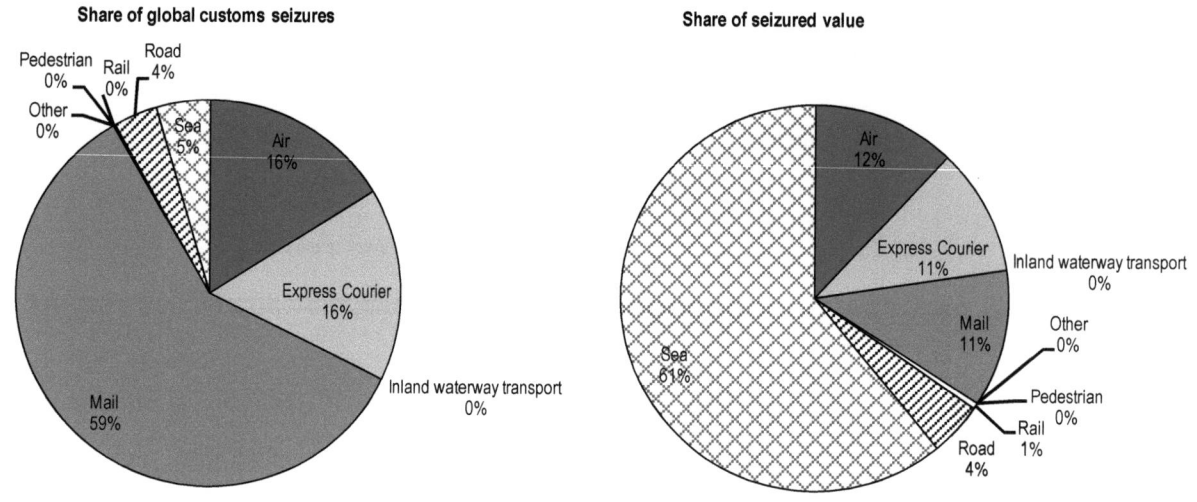

Source: OECD/EUIPO database.

Dangerous counterfeit goods shipped by vessel

This section concerns the shipment of dangerous fakes that are transported in container ships.

Impacted products

Figure 3.5 indicates that the toys and games (28%) were the most frequently seized product category by customs among dangerous fakes shipped by vessel from 2017 to 2019. They were followed by clothing (14%) footwear (12%) and electronic appliances (9%).

In terms of seized value, vehicles' parts were by far the most seized product category. This is partly due to one large seizure of more than 50 000 spare parts coming from China to Ukraine.

Figure 3.5. Main product categories of dangerous fakes shipped by vessel, 2017-19

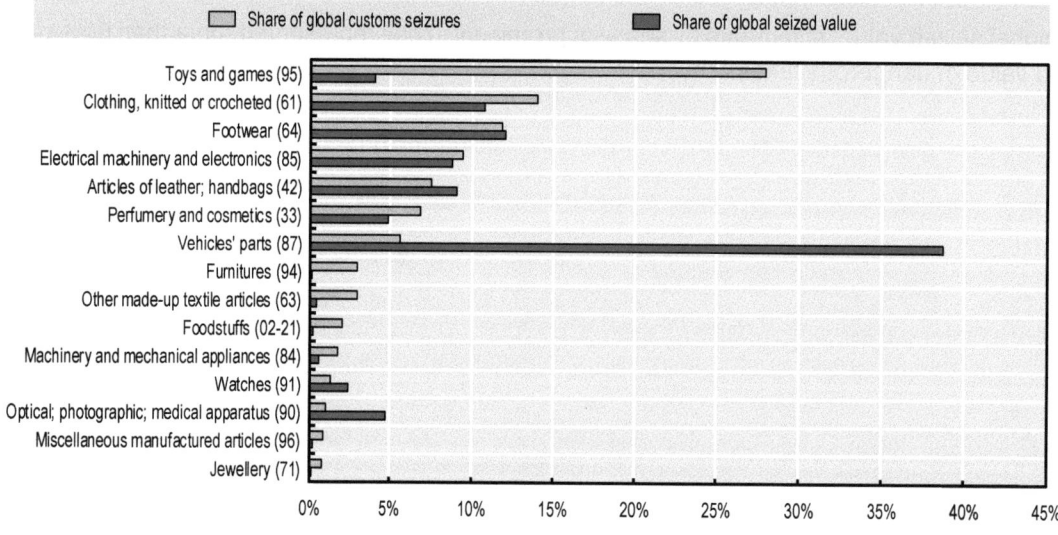

Source: OECD/EUIPO.

Trade routes

China was by far the main provenance economy of dangerous goods shipped by vessel from 2017-19, representing more than 70% of global customs seizures of these goods. As can be shown in Figure 3.6, Morocco (6%) plays an important role in trade in dangerous fakes shipped by vessel as it is the second provenance economy, followed by Turkey (4%).

Figure 3.6. Main provenance economies of dangerous fakes shipped by vessel, 2017-19

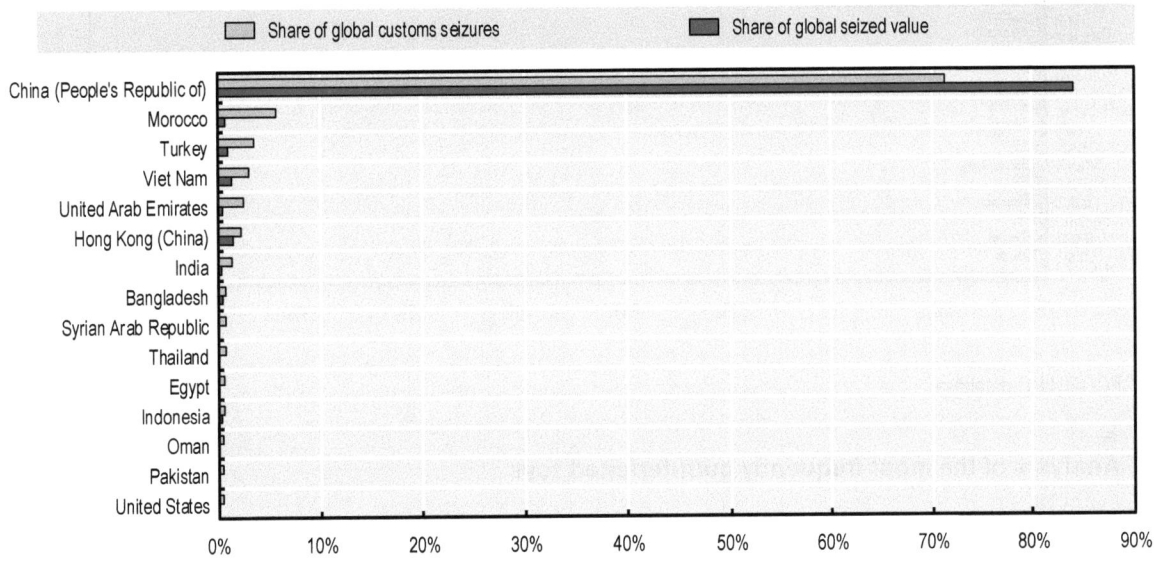

Source: OECD/EUIPO database.

The counterfeit dangerous goods shipped by sea were destined to Gulf countries, led by Saudi Arabia - which was the first destination for these goods, followed by Qatar and Kuwait (see Figure 3.7). The European Union countries (Poland, Spain, France, Hungary, and Germany) and South American countries (Chile, Dominican Republic) were also important outlets for dangerous fakes shipped by vessel from 2017 to 2019.

Figure 3.7. Main destination economies of dangerous fakes shipped by vessel, 2017-19

Share of global customs seizures
Share of global seized value
Saudi Arabia
Poland
Spain
Qatar
Chile
France
Hungary
Germany
Kuwait
United Kingdom
Russia
Bulgaria
Morocco
Romania
Czech Republic
Dominican Republic
Italy
Netherlands
Algeria
Albania
Libya
Belgium
Greece
Tunisia
Ukraine
0%
5%
10%
15%
20%
25%
30%
35%
40%
45%

Source: OECD/EUIPO database

Analysis of the most frequently counterfeited toys

As indicated by Figure 3.5 above, the toys and games were the most frequently seized products among dangerous fakes shipped by vessel. The customs seizures data indicate that building sets were the most frequently seized product by customs within this category.

Figure 3.8 which presents the main provenance-destination economies of the counterfeit building sets, indicates that China was the main provenance country while the Eastern European countries (Poland, Germany, Hungary and the Czech Republic) were the main destination economies.

Figure 3.8. Main provenance destination economies of the most frequently counterfeit dangerous goods (toys building set) shipped by vessel, 2017-19

Share of global seized value
Share of global customs seizures
60%
50%
40%
30%
20%
10%
0%
CHN-POL
CHN-DEU
CHN-HUN
CHN-CZE
CHN-ROU
CHN-LTU
CHN-BGR
CHN-FRA
CHN-BLR
CHN-GBR
CHN-NLD
CHN-CHL
CHN-CYP
CHN-ISL
HKG-EST
KOR-DEU

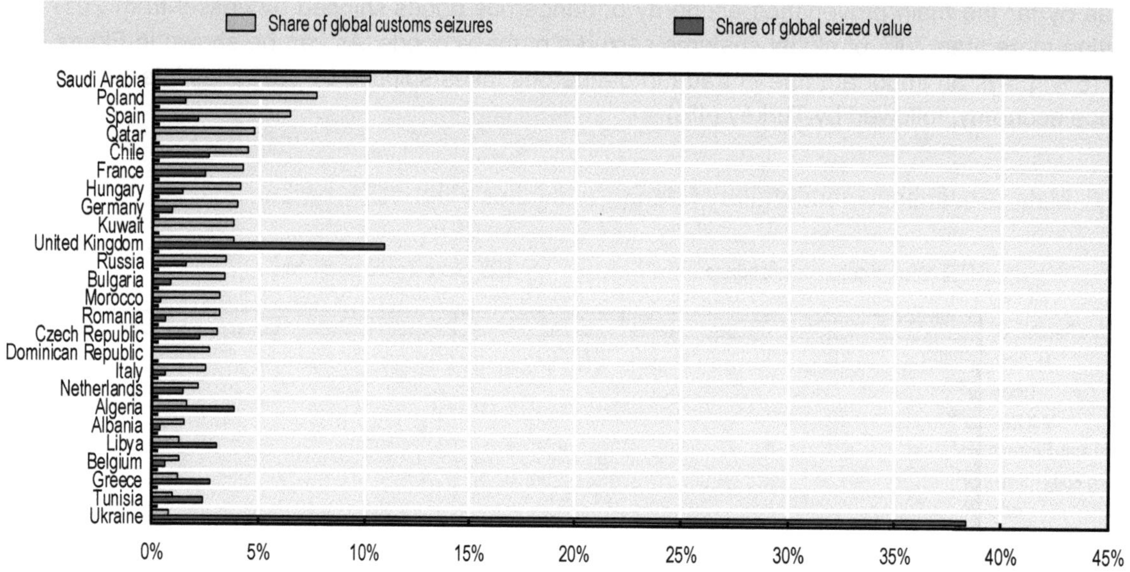

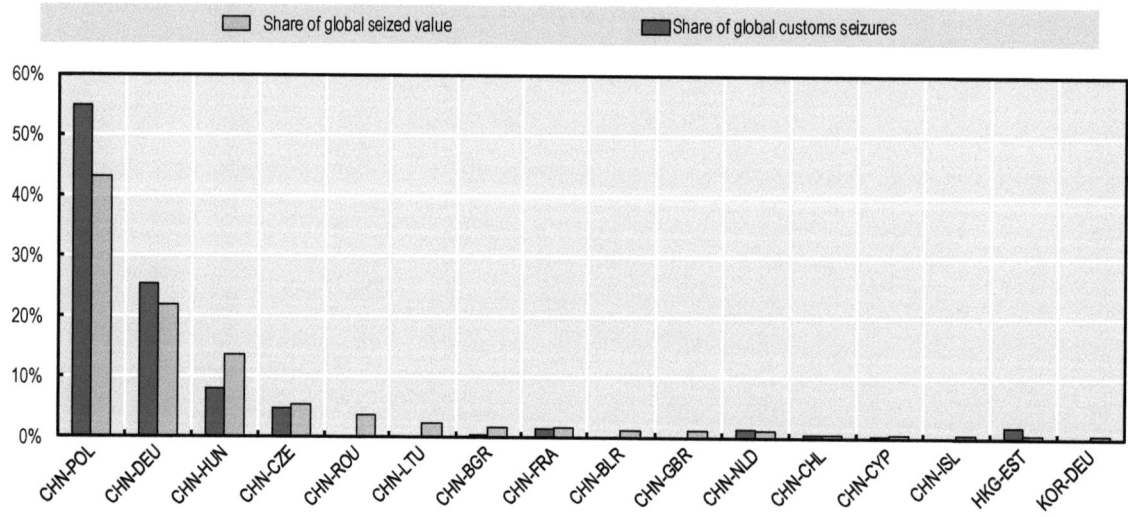

Source: OECD/EUIPO database.

The data on customs seizures reveal that the shipment size of fake toys tended to be large as almost a third of global customs seizures of these goods contained more than 500 items (see Figure 3.9).

Figure 3.9. Shipment size of the most frequently faked product (building set) shipped by vessel, 2017-19

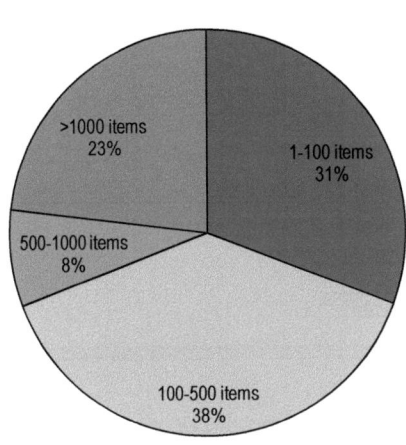

Source: OECD/EUIPO database.

Shipment size

Figure 3.10 presents the shipment size of global seizures of dangerous fakes from 2017 to 2019. It indicates that shipment size of these goods tended to be small as almost 60% of global seizures contained less than 6 items. Large shipments (i.e. more than 10 items) represented just over a third of the global seizures of dangerous fakes.

Figure 3.10. Shipment size of dangerous goods subject to counterfeiting, 2017-19

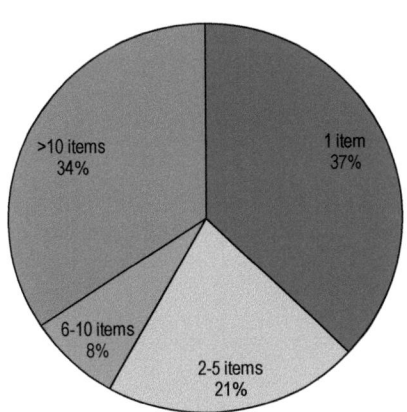

Source: OECD/EUIPO database.

Dangerous counterfeit goods transported by small parcels

This section concerns the shipment of dangerous fakes in small parcels (i.e. global seizures of dangerous fakes containing only one item).

Impacted products

Figure 3.11 indicates that among small parcels of dangerous fakes, footwear was the most frequently seized product from 2017 to 2019, equivalent to 35% of global customs seizures. It also included clothing (16%), leather goods (16%) and watches (9%).

Figure 3.11. Main product categories of small parcels of dangerous fakes, 2017-19

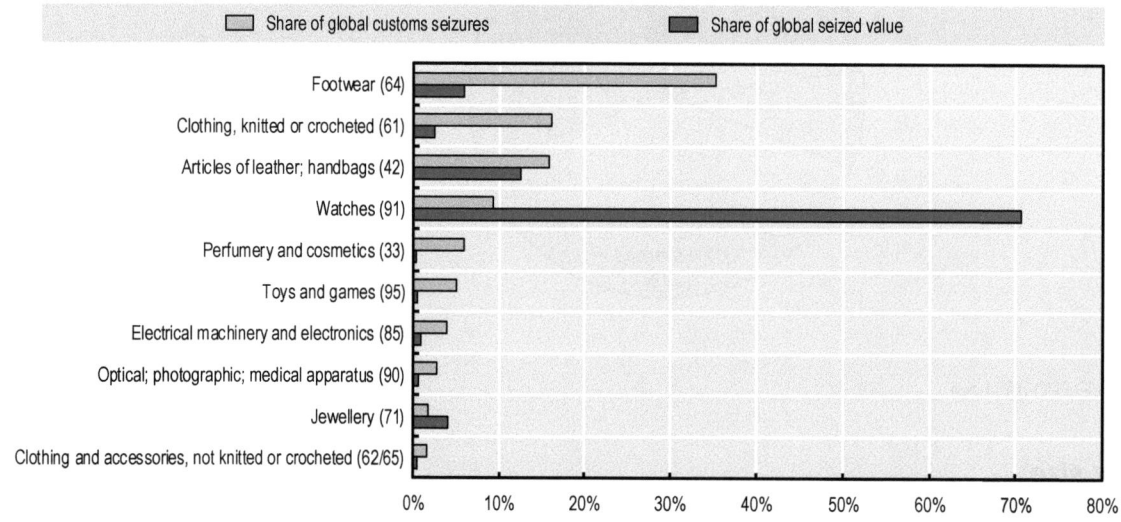

Source: OECD/EUIPO database.

Trade routes

The dangerous fakes shipped through small parcels mainly came from the main providers of counterfeit goods such as China (63% of global customs seizures), Hong Kong (China) (20%), Turkey (6%) and Singapore (2%).

Figure 3.12. Main provenance economies of small parcels of dangerous fakes, 2017-19

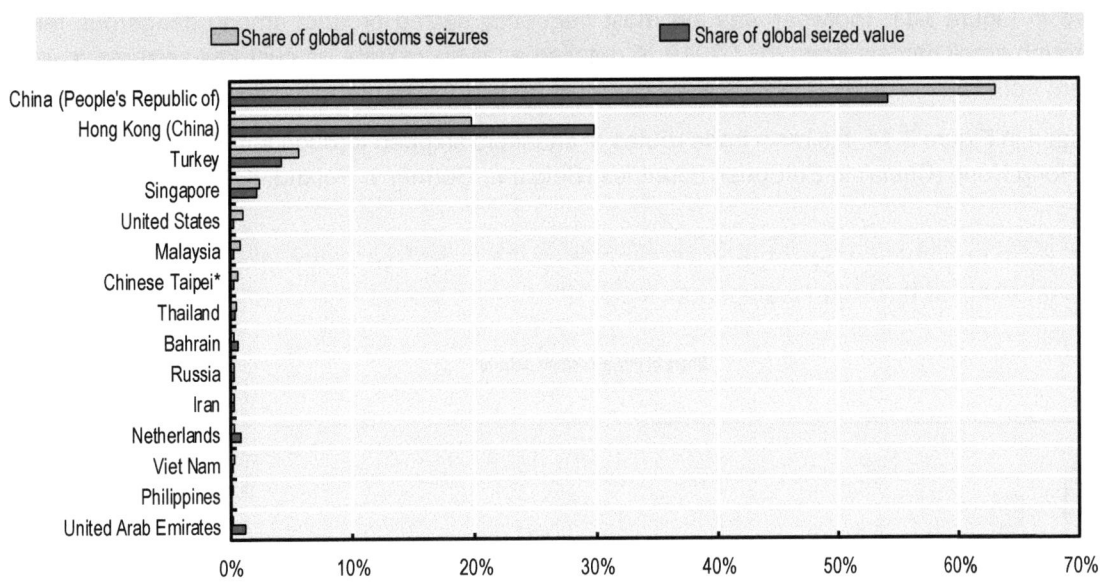

Source: OECD/EUIPO database.

European countries and the United States were the main destination economies of the small parcels containing dangerous goods. As indicated in Figure 3.13, Germany (30% of global seizures of small parcels of dangerous goods), the United States (26%), Belgium (15%) and Italy (7%) were the principal destinations of dangerous goods shipped through small parcels from 2017 to 2019.

Figure 3.13. Main destination economies of small parcels of dangerous fakes, 2017-19

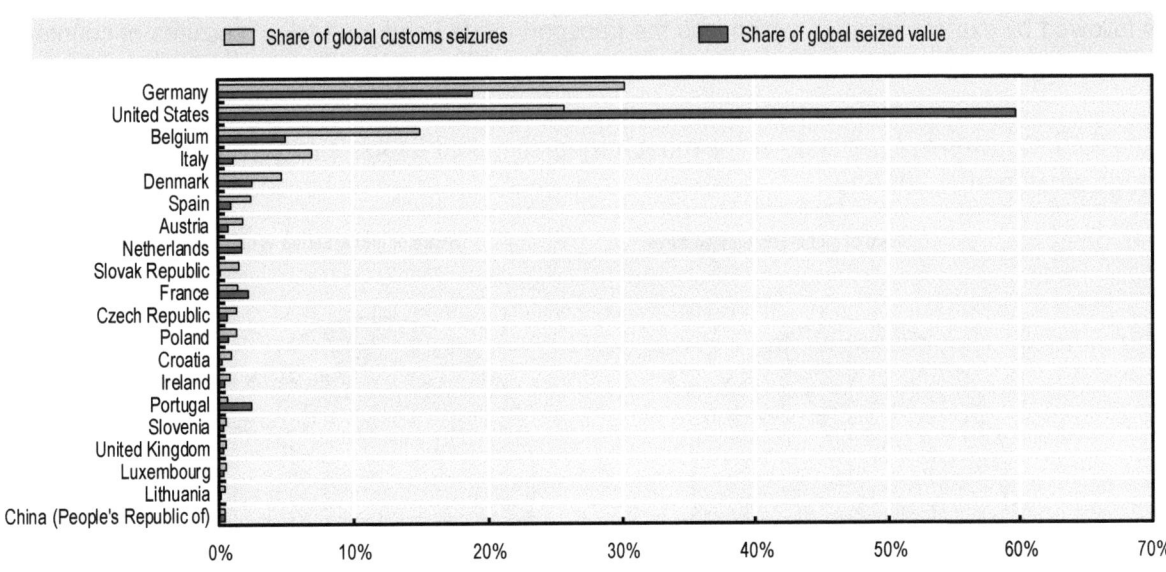

Source: OECD/EUIPO database.

Analysis of the most frequently counterfeited footwear

As indicated in Figure 3.11, footwear was the most frequently seized product among dangerous fakes shipped through small parcels from 2017-2019. A detailed analysis of data on customs seizures reveals that sneakers from two major sport brands were the most frequently counterfeited items in this category.

As can be seen in Figure 3.14, the main trade routes of sneakers shipped through small parcels were from China and Hong Kong (China) to European countries (Belgium, Germany, Poland, Italy).

Figure 3.14. Main provenance-destination economies of the most frequently faked dangerous good (sports shoes) shipped through small parcel, 2017-19

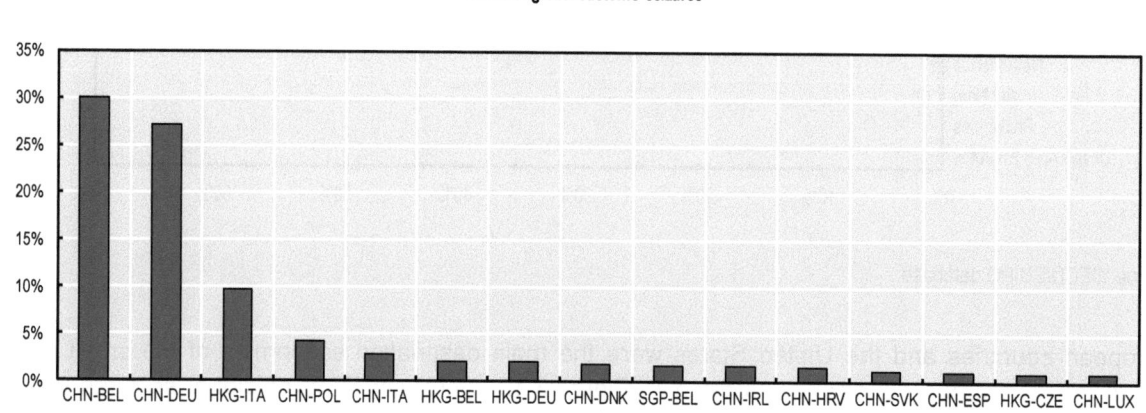

Source: OECD/EUIPO database.

In terms of both global seized value (81%) and the number of customs seizures (73%), the postal service was by far the most used to ship fake sneakers via small parcels from 2017 to 2019 (see Figure 3.15). It was followed by express courrier, which was the transport mode used for 14% of seizures of counterfeit sneakers shipped via small parcels.

Figure 3.15. Conveyance methods of the most frequently faked dangerous good (sneaker) shipped through small parcel, 2017-19

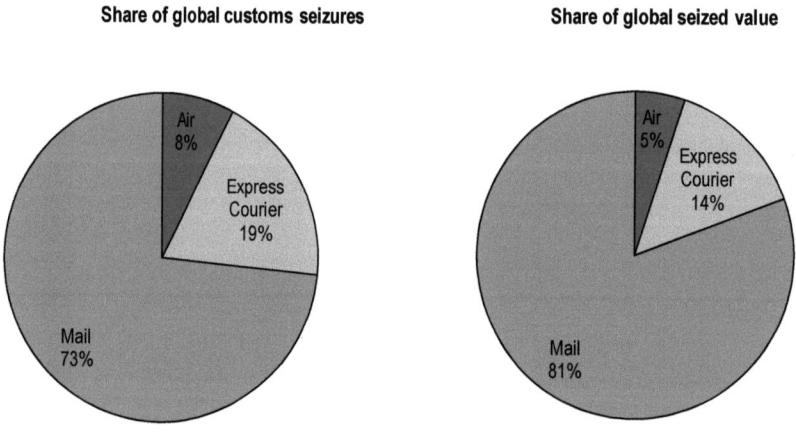

Source: OECD/EUIPO database.

EU Case Study

This section focuses on trade of dangerous fakes destined for the EU 28 markets. The United Kingdom is included to the scope as the reference period (2017-19) is prior to the Brexit.

At the EU level, there were almost 230 000 seizures of dangerous goods from 2017 to 2019 which came from almost 170 different provenance economies.

Dangerous product categories subject to counterfeiting

From 2017 to 2019, footwear (31%) was the most frequently seized dangerous good destined for the EU (see Figure 3.16). It was followed by clothing (23%) and leather goods (9%). This top 3 is the same at the worldwide level. However, toys and games and cosmetics, which are the other most frequently seized products, seem to be more important at the EU level than at worldwide level.

As in the worldwide case, the dangerous product categories subject to counterfeiting are numerous and varied ranging from common goods to pharmaceuticals and machinery.

Figure 3.16. Main product categories of dangerous counterfeit goods imported into the EU, 2017-19

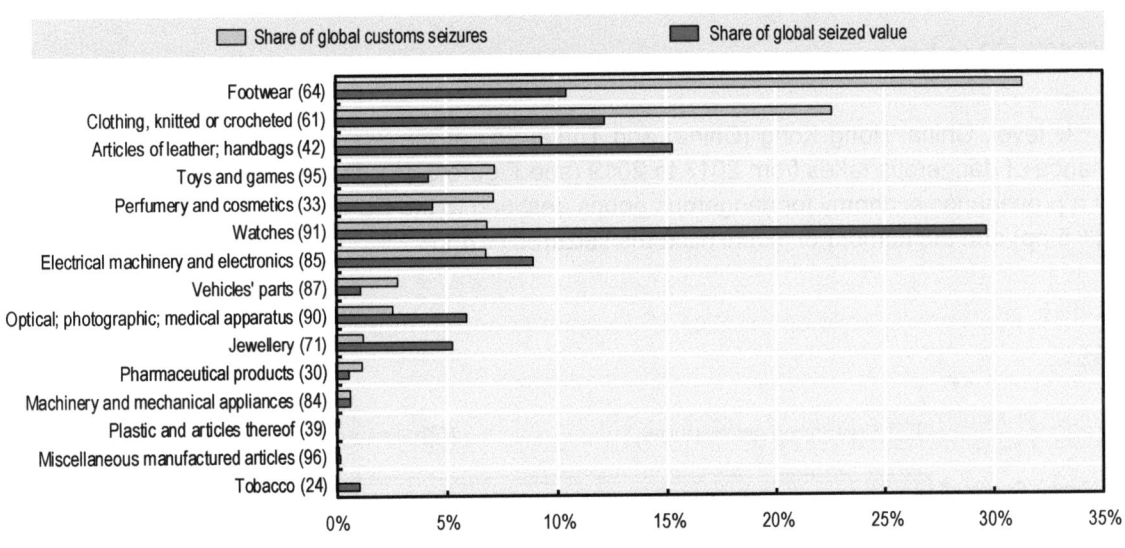

Source: OECD/EUIPO database.

Main trade routes of trade in dangerous fakes destined to the EU countries

Germany (35% of global customs seizures of dangerous products), Belgium (16%), Italy (9%), Denmark (5%) and Spain (5%) were the most targeted EU countries as they were the most frequently reported as destination economies for these products (see Figure 3.17).

Figure 3.17. Main destination economies of dangerous counterfeit goods imported into the EU, 2017-19

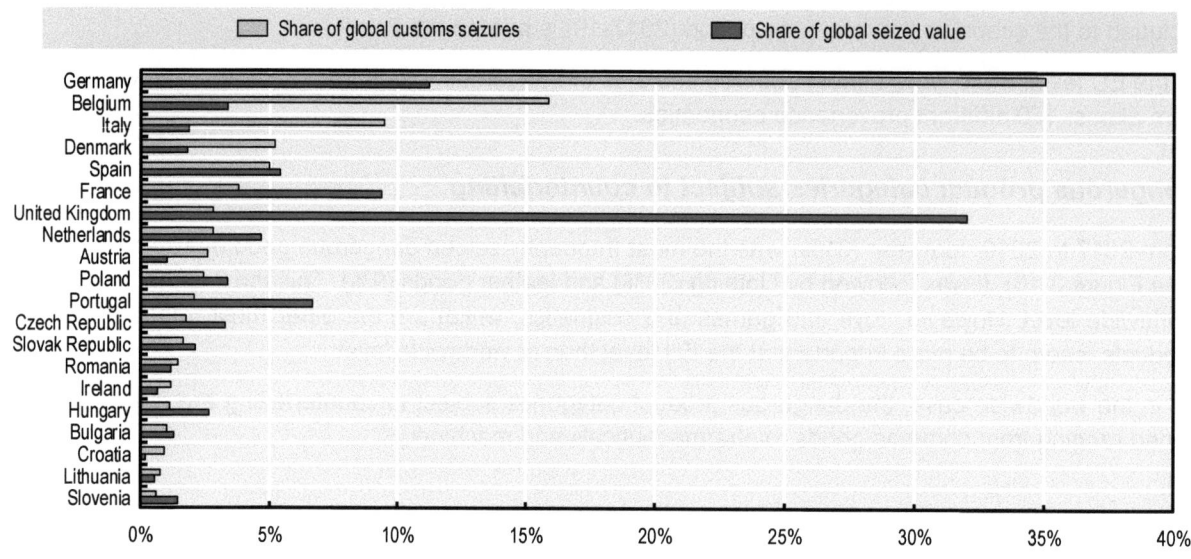

Source: OECD/EUIPO database.

At the EU level, China, Hong Kong (China) and Turkey, as at the worldwide level, were also the main provenance of dangerous fakes from 2017 to 2019 (see Figure 3.18). Turkey, however, played a greater role as a provenance economy for dangerous goods destined to the EU in terms of both the global seized value (+ 5 pp) and the number of global customs seizures (+ 4pp).

Figure 3.18. Main provenance economies of dangerous counterfeit goods imported into the EU, 2017-19

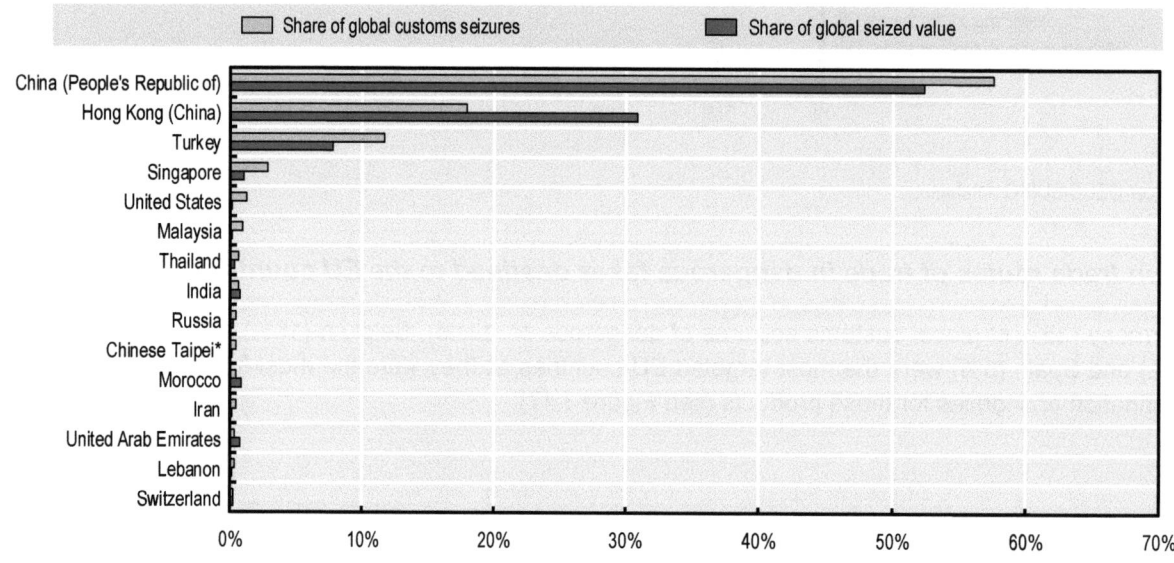

Source: OECD/EUIPO database.

Transport modes of dangerous goods destined to the EU countries

At the EU level, the postal service was also the preferred transport mode for shipping dangerous fakes during 2017-19, representing 61% of global customs seizures of dangerous products destined to the EU (see Figure 3.19). It was followed by express courrier (17%) and air (16%).

In terms of global seized value, the picture at the EU level differs from that at the international level. Sea represented 38% of global seized value of dangerous fakes destined to the EU while it represented 61% at the international level.

Figure 3.19. Conveyance methods of dangerous counterfeit goods imported into the EU, 2017-19

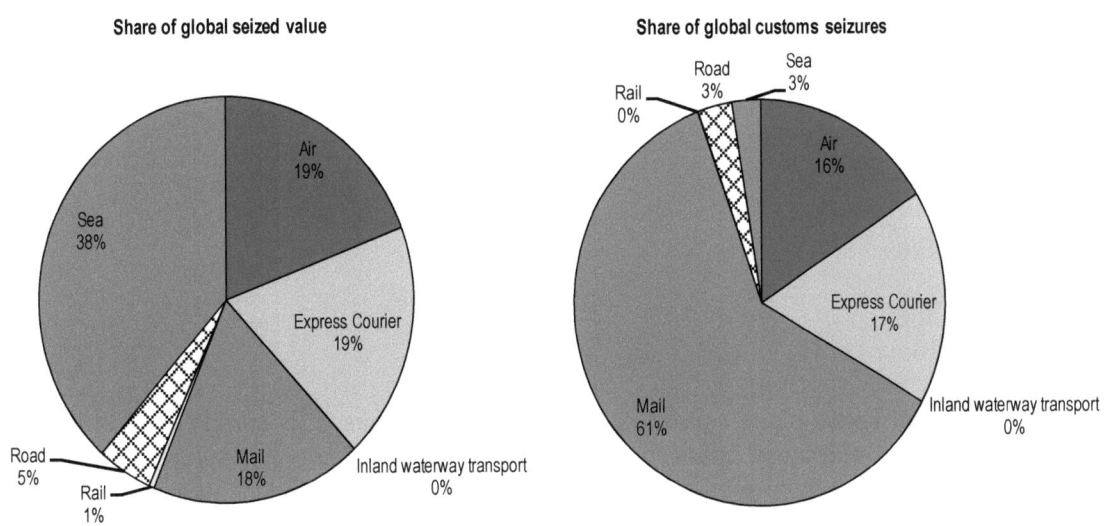

Source: OECD/EUIPO database.

At the EU level, the average shipment size of dangerous fakes is smaller than at the international level. The lesser role of transport by vessel in European countries may be an explanation. Small parcels largely dominated as they represented 62% of global customs seizures of dangerous products destined to the EU (compared to 47% at the international level). The large shipments (i.e. more than 10 items) represented only 15% of global seizures of dangerous goods (compared to 26% at the international level).

Figure 3.20. Shipment size of dangerous counterfeit goods imported into the EU, 2017-19

Share of global customs seizures

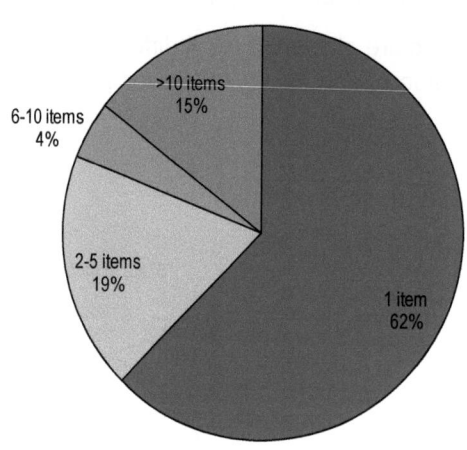

Source: OECD/EUIPO database.

Focused scope

The focused approach takes into account the most dangerous types of counterfeit goods: foodstuffs, pharmaceutical products and those goods' categories, that are most frequently subject to safety alerts. This is established using the databases on product safety problems and product recalls. In particular, as discussed in Chapter two, this section uses the main products subject to alert in the EU Safety Gate system. This scope includes the following product categories (HS code):

- Foodstuffs (02-21)
- Pharmaceutical products (30)
- Perfumery and cosmetics (33)
- Soap (34)
- Clothing, knitted or crocheted (61)
- Other made-up textile articles (63)
- Jewellery (71)
- Electrical machinery and electronics (85)
- Vehicles' parts (87)
- Watches (91)
- Toys and games (95)

Specifically, pharmaceuticals, foodstuffs and cosmetics have been included in whole, at a two digit level, as structured interviews with enforcement officials underscored the wide presence of risky goods in these categories. For all other categories, only some subcategories of products at four-digit level were included, based on the specific indications in the Safety Gate database. These subcategories are listed below:

- Soap (34)
  - HS 3402: Organic surface-active agents (not soap); surface-active, washing (including auxiliary washing) and cleaning preparations, containing soap or not, excluding those of heading n°. 3401

- Clothing, knitted or crocheted (61)
    - HS 6101: Coats; men's or boys' overcoats, car-coats, capes, cloaks, anoraks, ski-jackets, wind-cheaters, wind-jackets and similar articles; knitted or crocheted, other than those of heading n°. 6103
    - HS 6102: Coats; women's or girls' overcoats, car-coats, capes, cloaks, anoraks, ski-jackets, wind-cheaters, wind-jackets and similar articles, knitted or crocheted, other than those of heading n°. 6104
    - HS 6104: Suits, ensembles, jackets, dresses, skirts, divided skirts, trousers, bib and brace overalls, breeches and shorts (not swimwear), women's or girls', knitted or crocheted
    - HS 6105: Shirts; men's or boys', knitted or crocheted
- Other made-up textile articles (63)
    - HS 6307: Textiles; made up articles not eslsewhere specified (n.e.s). in chapter 63, including dress patterns
- Jewellery (71)
    - HS 7116: Articles of natural or cultured pearls, precious or semi-precious stones (natural, synthetic or reconstructed)
- Electrical machinery and electronics (85)
    - HS 8504: Electric transformers, static converters (eg rectifiers) and inductors
    - HS 8516: Electric water, space, soil heaters; electro-thermic hair-dressing apparatus; hand dryers, irons; electro-thermic appliances for domestic purposes; electro heating resistors, not of heading n° 8545
    - HS 8539: Lamps; electric filament or discharge lamps, including sealed beam lamp units and ultra-violet or infra-red lamps, arc-lamps
- Vehicles' parts (87)
    - HS 8703: Motor cars and other motor vehicles; principally designed for the transport of persons (other than those of heading n°. 8702), including station wagons and racing cars
    - HS 8711: Motorcycles (including mopeds) and cycles; fitted with an auxiliary motor, with or without side-cars; side-cars
- Watches (91)
    - HS 9113: Watch straps, watch bands, watch bracelets and parts thereof
- Toys and games (95)
    - HS 9503: Tricycles, scooters, pedal cars and similar wheeled toys; dolls' carriages; dolls; other toys; reduced-size (scale) models and similar recreational models, working or not; puzzles of all kinds
    - HS 9506: Gymnastics, athletics, other sports (including table tennis) or outdoor games equipment, n.e.s. in the chapter 95, swimming pools and paddling pools

While risks for consumers posed by foodstuffs, pharmaceuticals, cosmetics, electrical machinery and electronics, vehicles' parts and toys and games are quite clear those associated with categories such as clothing, textiles, jewellery and watches are less obvious. The risks associated with these categories are discussed in Chapter 1 and notably illustrated in Table 1.6. However, it is important to highlight that cases of jewellery containing toxic substances as heavy metals like lead and cadmium, as well as PVC and other plastics have been reported. The main area of concern for watches are dangerous chemicals and toxic heavy metals used for production of strap and watch case. Clothing and textiles may contain toxic materials, or made in a ways that poses risks of chocking or fire. For example, a case of a cushion cover that was made out of extremely toxic textile material containing dyes releasing the aromatic amine benzidine has been reported. In direct and prolonged contact with the skin, this aromatic amine may be absorbed by the skin causing cancer, cell mutations and affect reproduction.

There were just over 70 000 customs seizures of potential dangerous goods from 2017 to 2019 in the HS categories covered. The seizures originated in 170 economies, and were shipped to 115 economies.

Trade volumes

According to the GTRIC methodology, the total volume of potential dangerous fakes traded amounted to almost USD 75 billion in 2019. As can be seen in Figure 3.21, the value of global trade in dangerous fakes were slightly higher in 2017 and 2018, and amounted to USD 88.4 billion.

The trade in dangerous fakes represented a third of global trade in counterfeit goods within the focused scope in 2019. When considering the global value of trade in fakes (i.e. all goods categories) which has been estimated to USD 464 billion in a previous OECD/EUIPO report (Global Trade in Fakes : A Worrying Threat), the trade of potential dangerous fakes accounted for 16% of global trade in counterfeit goods overall the same year.

Figure 3.21. Estimates of global trade in dangerous fakes, 2017-19

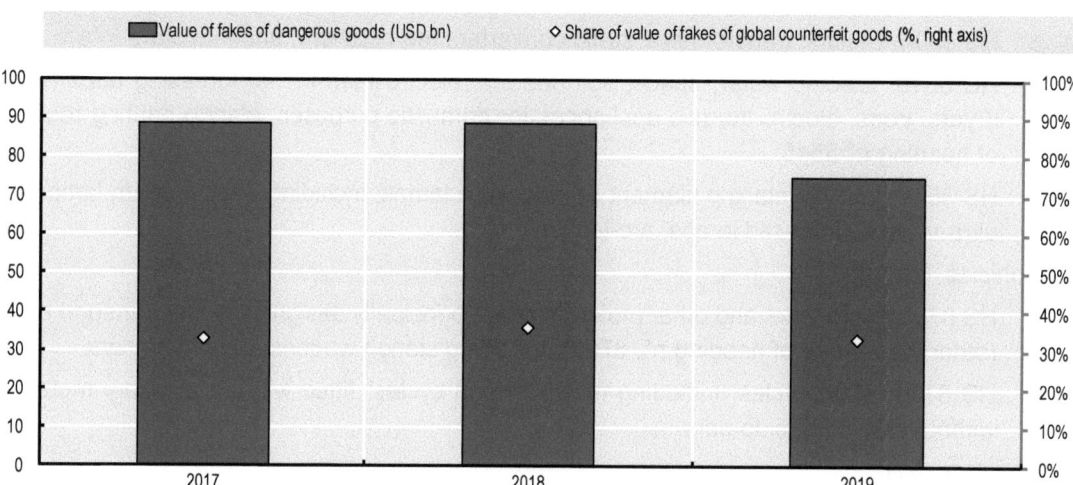

Note: The share was based on the value of fakes of all counterfeit goods in categories within the focused scope (foodstuffs, pharmaceuticals, cosmetics, soap, clothing, textiles, jewellery, electronic appliances, vehicles' parts watches as well as toys and games).
Source: OECD/EUIPO database.

Trade routes

Figure 3.22 indicates that the main provenance of dangerous fakes indicates that dangerous fakes are the same as those for global counterfeit goods overall.

The list of dangerous counterfeit goods is broad and many Asian countries are included, led by China (55% of global customs seizures) and Hong Kong (China) (19%). In addition to Asian countries, Turkey (9%) was also an important provider of dangerous fake products.

Figure 3.22. Main provenance economies of dangerous fakes, 2017-19

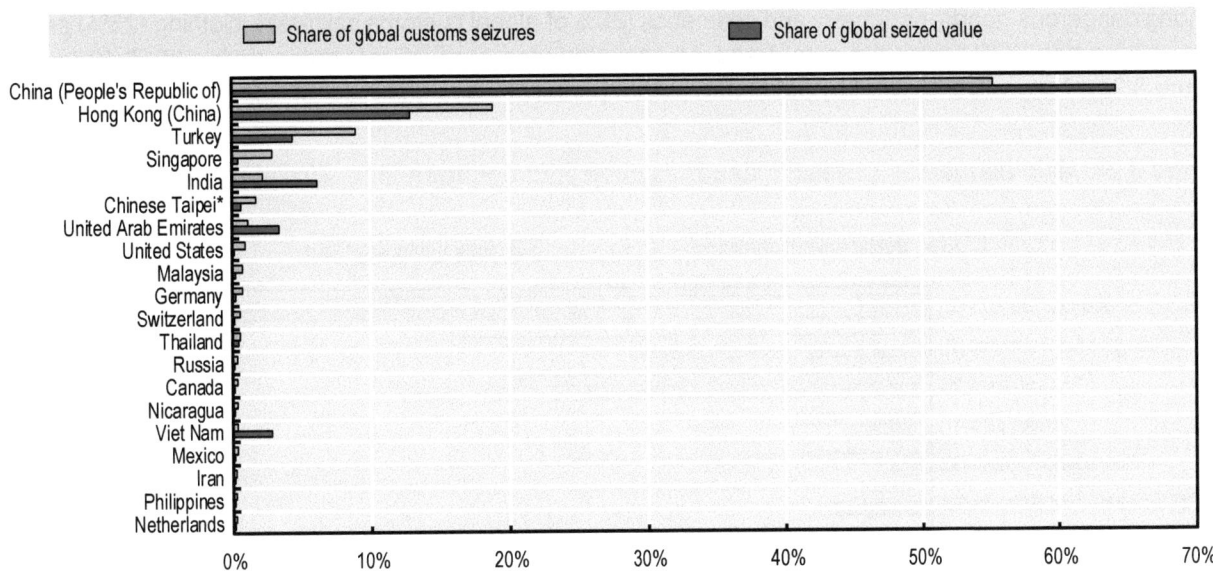

Source: OECD/EUIPO database.

As indicated in Figure 3.23, from 2017 to 2019, the dangerous counterfeit products were mainly destined to Germany (34% of global customs seizures of dangerous fakes) and the United States (23%). Many European Union countries are included in the top destinations of dangerous fakes; Belgium accounted for 7% of seizures, followed by, Denmark (4%), Italy (3%) and Spain (2.6%).

Figure 3.23. Main destination economies of dangerous fakes, 2017-19

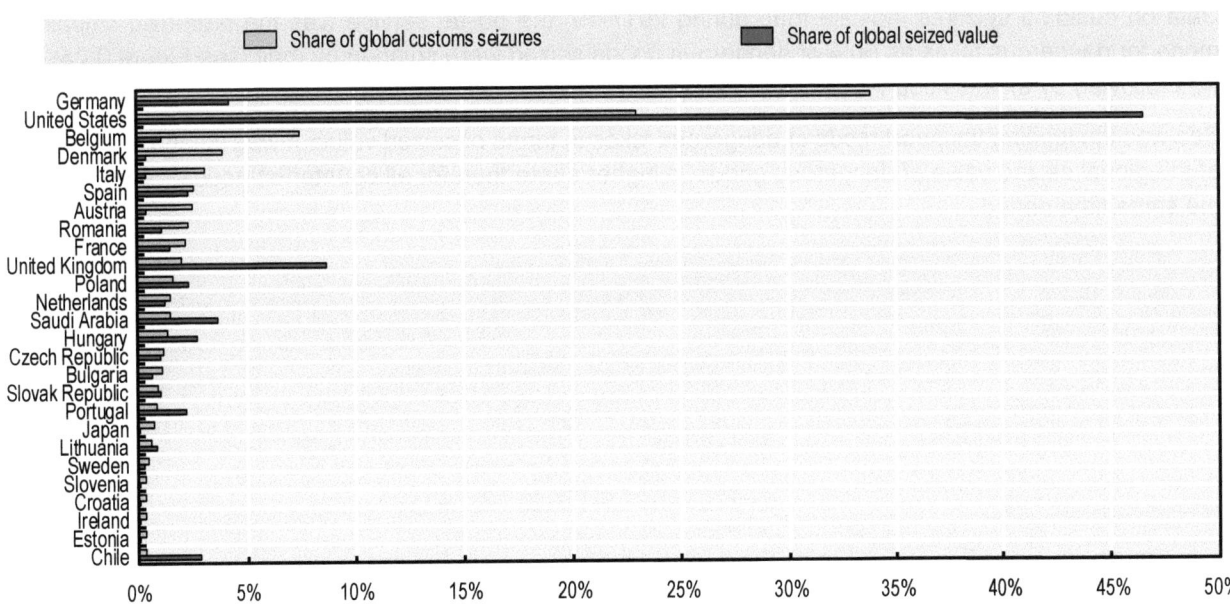

Source: OECD/EUIPO database.

Products impacted

Among dangerous goods, perfumery and cosmetics (32% of global customs seizures), clothing (25%) and toys and games (22%) were the most frequently counterfeited product categories during 2017-19 (see Figure 3.24). They were followed by automotive spare parts (7%) and pharmaceuticals (5%).

Figure 3.24. Main dangerous product categories subject to counterfeiting, 2017-19

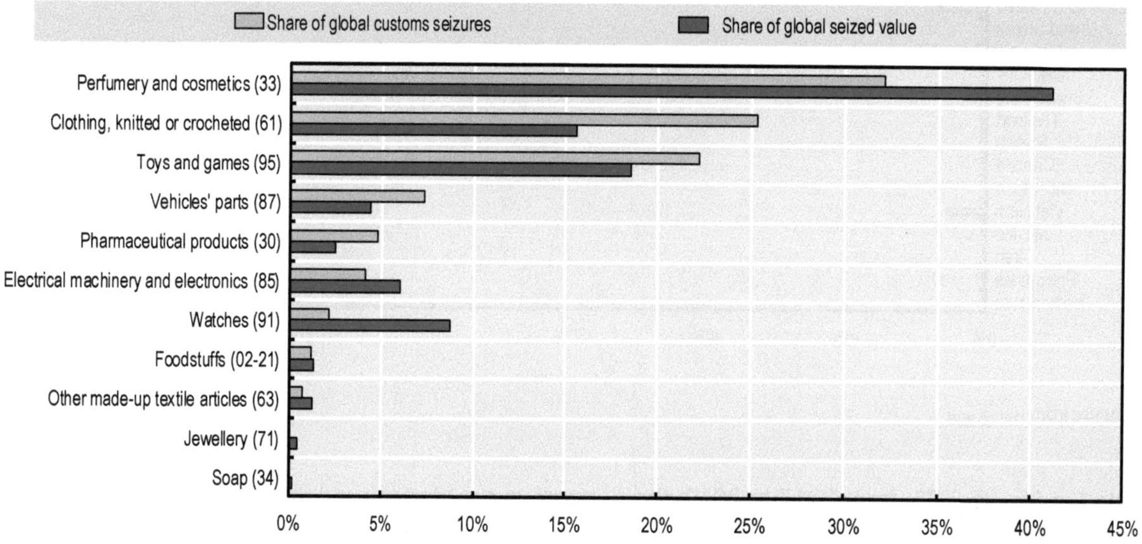

Source: OECD/EUIPO database.

Transport methods of dangerous fakes

Data on customs seizures indicate that, during 2017-19, the postal service was the preferred shipping mode for dangerous fakes as 60% of dangerous goods seized were shipped by mail (see Figure 3.25). It was followed by express courier (14%) and air (12%).

Sea was the leading transport mode of dangerous fakes in terms of seized value. It was equivalent to 64% of the global seized value of dangerous goods, a higher share than for all counterfeit goods (53%) during the same time period.

Figure 3.25. Conveyance methods of dangerous goods subject to counterfeiting, 2017-19

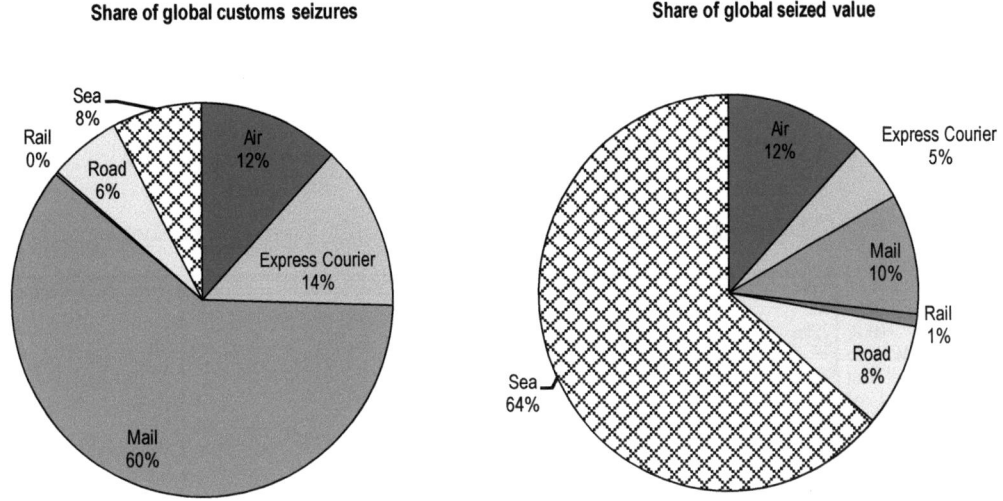

Source: OECD/EUIPO database.

Dangerous counterfeit goods shipped by vessel

The following section focuses on seizures of dangerous fakes shipped in containers.

Impacted products

Among the seized dangerous fakes shipped by vessel, toys and games were the most frequently counterfeited products, equivalent to 53% of the global customs seizures of containerized dangerous goods (see Figure 3.26). It was followed by cosmetics (20%), clothing (9%) and automotive spare parts (8%).

Figure 3.26. Main product categories of dangerous fake goods shipped by vessel, 2017-19

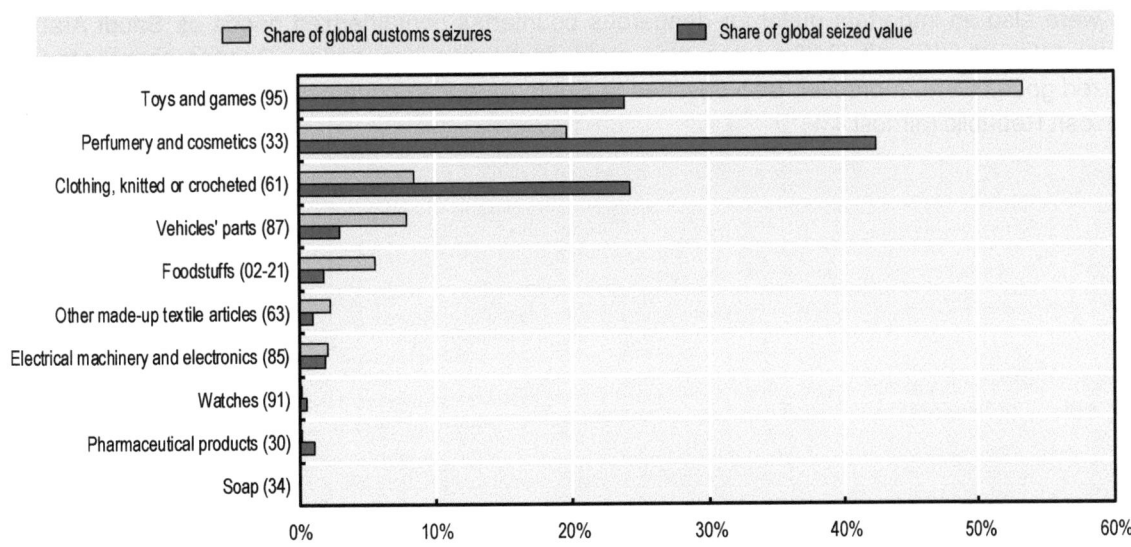

Source: OECD/EUIPO database.

DANGEROUS FAKES © OECD/EUIPO 2022

Trade routes

As indicated in Figure 3.27, the containerized counterfeit dangerous goods came mainly from China (77% of global customs seizures of dangerous fakes), the United Arab Emirates (3%), Turkey (3%) and Morocco (2%).

Figure 3.27. Main provenance economies of dangerous fake goods shipped by vessel, 2017-19

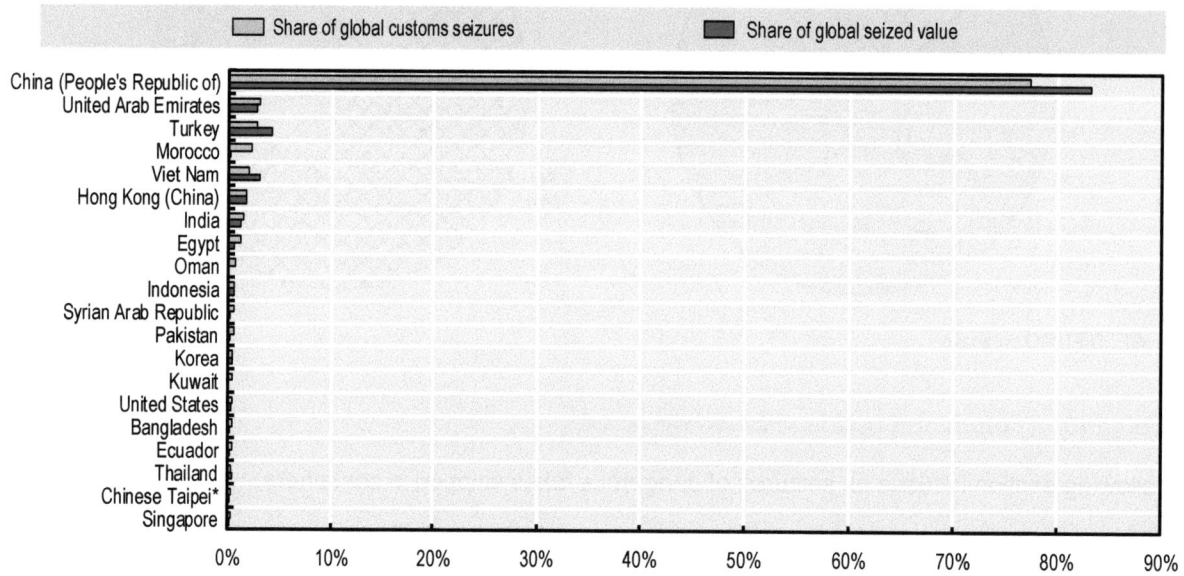

Source: OECD/EUIPO database.

Data on customs seizures also reveal that the list of destination economies of containerized dangerous fakes is very broad (see Figure 3.28). During 2017-19, European countries (particularly Eastern European countries) were an important destination for containerized dangerous fakes, led by Poland (12% of global seizures of containerized dangerous fakes), Hungary (6%), Romania (4%) and Germany (4%). The Gulf countries were also an important outlet for dangerous counterfeit containerized goods as Saudi Arabia (7%), Qatar (4%) and Kuwait (3.6%) were also main destination economies. Dangerous counterfeit containerized goods were, moreover, also destined to South American countries, notably Chile (5%) and the Dominican Republic (almost 1%).

Figure 3.28. Main destination economies of dangerous fake goods shipped by vessel, 2017-19

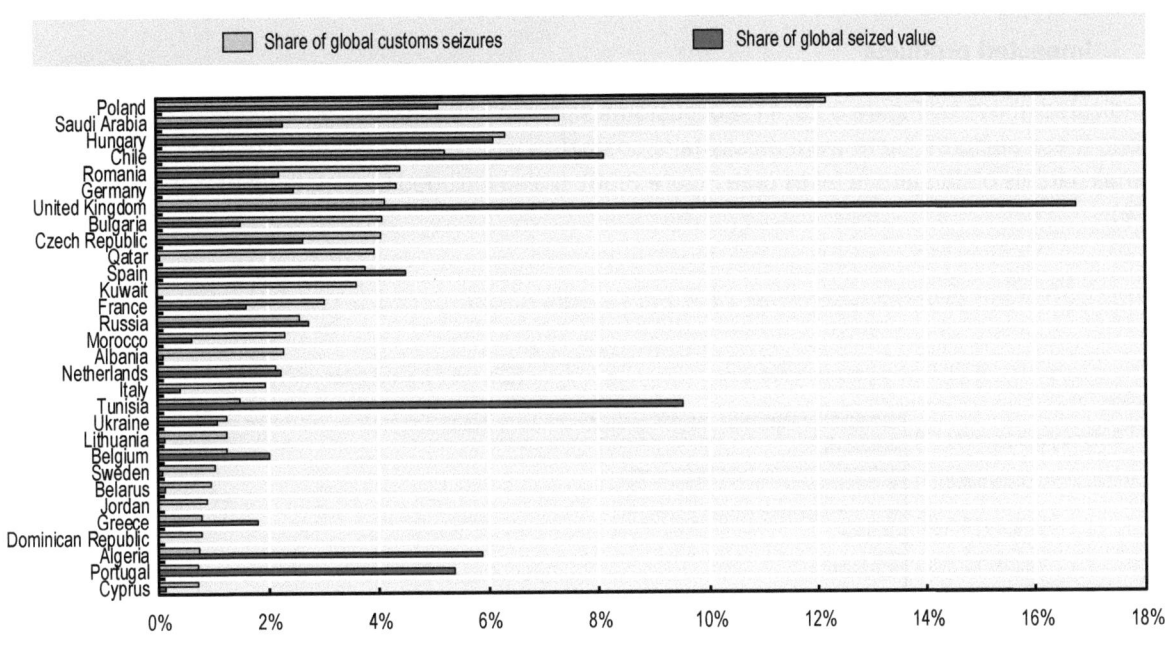

Source: OECD/EUIPO database.

Shipment size of dangerous fakes

Figure 3.29 indicates that the shipment size of all dangerous fakes within the focused scope seized tended to be small during 2017-19; shipments containing less than 10 items represented 64% of global seizures of dangerous goods while it represented 61% of seizures of all counterfeit goods.

Figure 3.29. Shipment size of dangerous goods seized, 2017-19

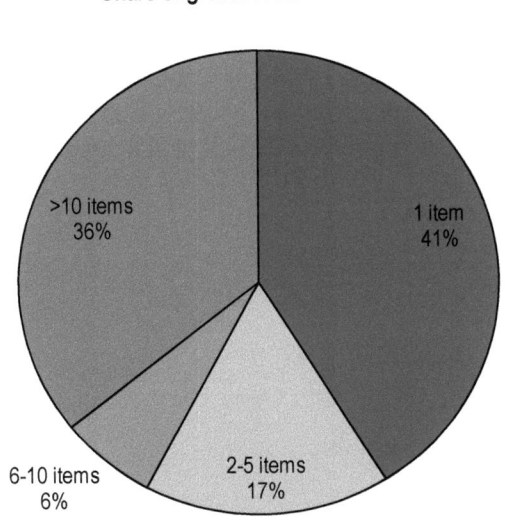

Source: OECD/EUIPO.

Dangerous counterfeit goods shipped by parcels

The following paragraph focuses on analysing the seizures of dangerous goods sent by small parcels.

Impacted products

As indicated above by Figure 3.29, 41% of customs seizures of dangerous goods contained only one item. Among these seizures, there were mostly fake cosmetics which accounted for 42% of the global seizures of small parcels of dangerous fakes (see Figure 3.30). It also included fake clothing (24%), toys and games (24%).

Figure 3.30. Main product categories of small parcels of dangerous fakes, 2017-19

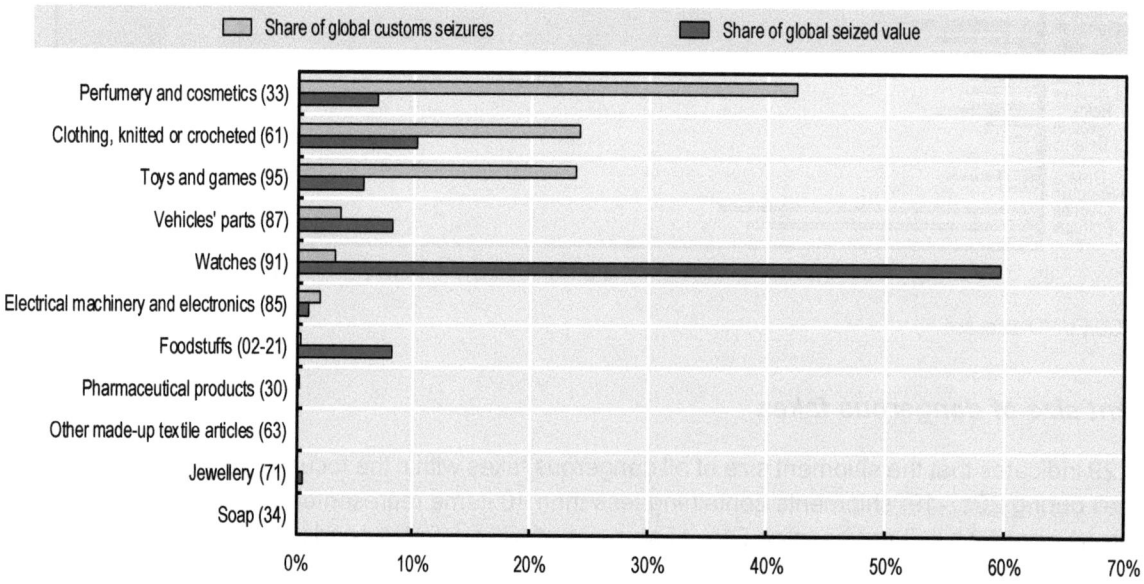

Source: OECD/EUIPO database.

Trade routes

Figure 3.31 shows that dangerous fakes shipped through small parcels came from China (75%), Hong Kong (China) (10%) Turkey (5%) and Singapore (2%), which are the leading sources of all counterfeit goods. Altogether, these four countries accounted for 92% of global customs seizures of dangerous fakes shipped via small parcels.

Figure 3.31. Main provenance economies of small parcels of dangerous fakes, 2017-19

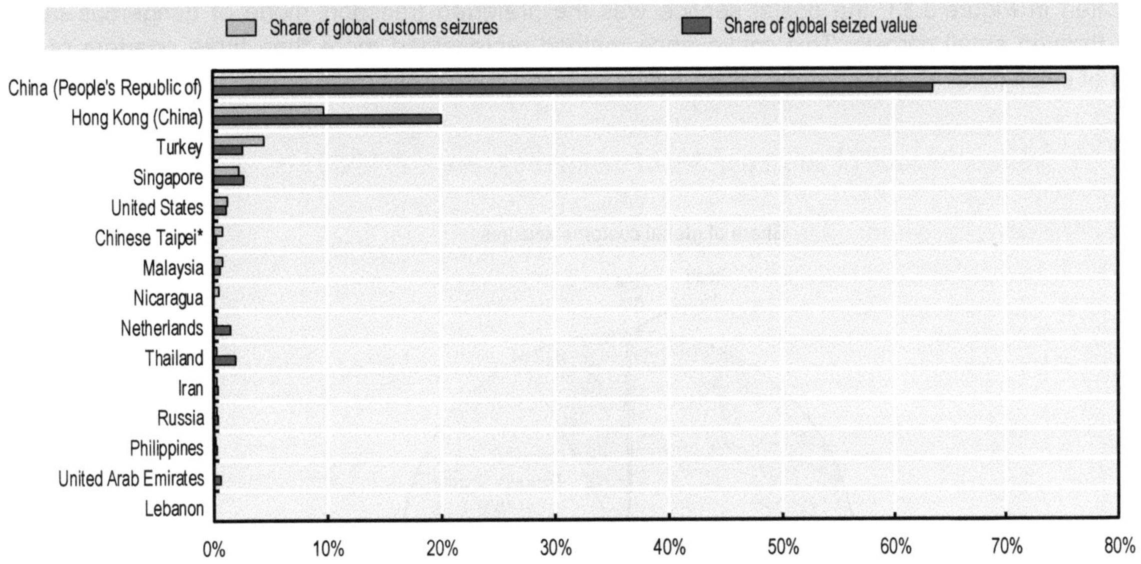

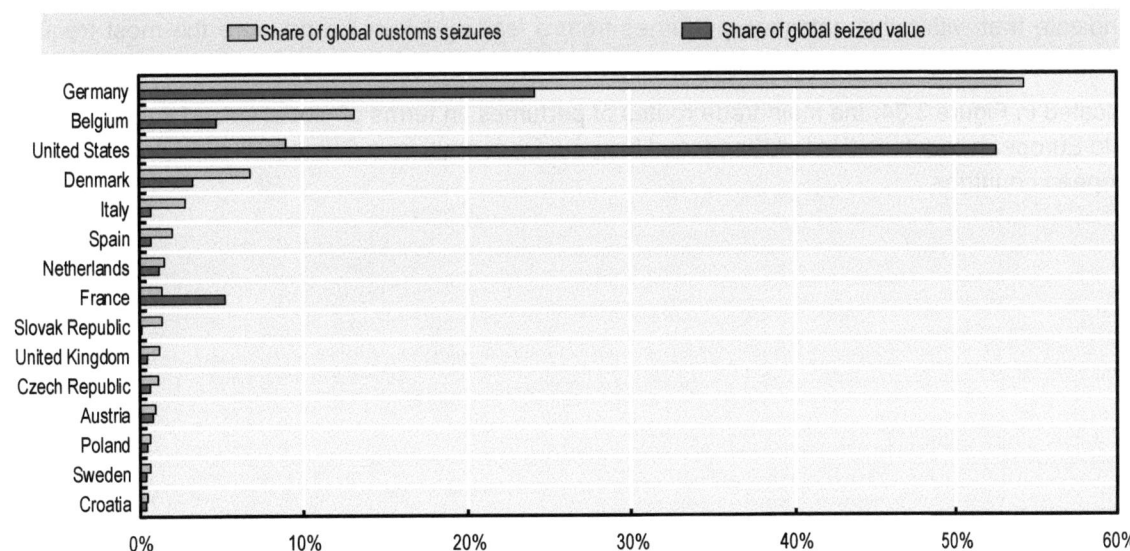

Source: OECD/EUIPO database.

The customs seizures data show that small parcels of dangerous fakes were mainly destined to developed countries (European countries and the United States) with Germany (54%), Belgium (13%), the United States (9%), and Denmark (7%) being the most frequent destination economies (see Figure 3.32).

The United States played a key role in terms of global seized value, representing more than half of seized value of dangerous goods sent through small parcels.

Figure 3.32. Main destination economies of small parcels of dangerous fakes, 2017-19

Source: OECD/EUIPO database.

DANGEROUS FAKES © OECD/EUIPO 2022

Transport mode

As indicated in Figure 3.33, the postal service was the preferred transport mode of dangerous fakes shipped through small parcels. This conveyance method represented more than three quarters of the seizures of small parcels of dangerous fakes. It was followed by express courrier (15%) and air (8%).

Figure 3.33. Transport mode of small parcels of dangerous fakes, 2017-19

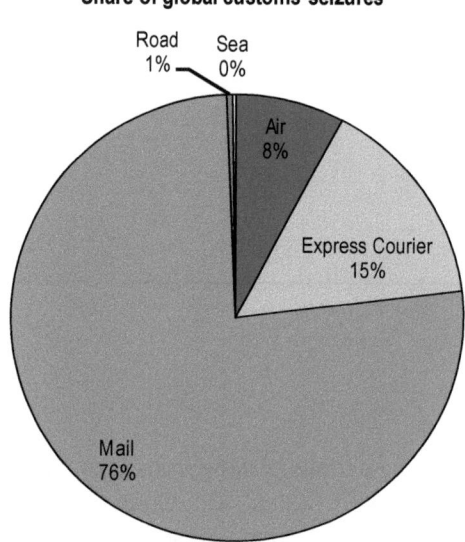

Source: OECD/EUIPO database.

Analysis of the most frequently counterfeited cosmetics

Cosmetics were the most frequently seized products among the small parcels of dangerous fakes. The data indicate that within this category, perfumes from a leading luxury brand were the most frequently counterfeited products sent by small parcels.

As indicated in Figure 3.34, the main trade routes of perfumes, in terms of global seized value, were from China to European countries (United Kingdom, Hungary, Germany), from China to Tunisia and from Turkey to European countries.

Figure 3.34. Main provenance-destination economies of the most frequently faked product (perfumes) sent via small parcels, 2017-19

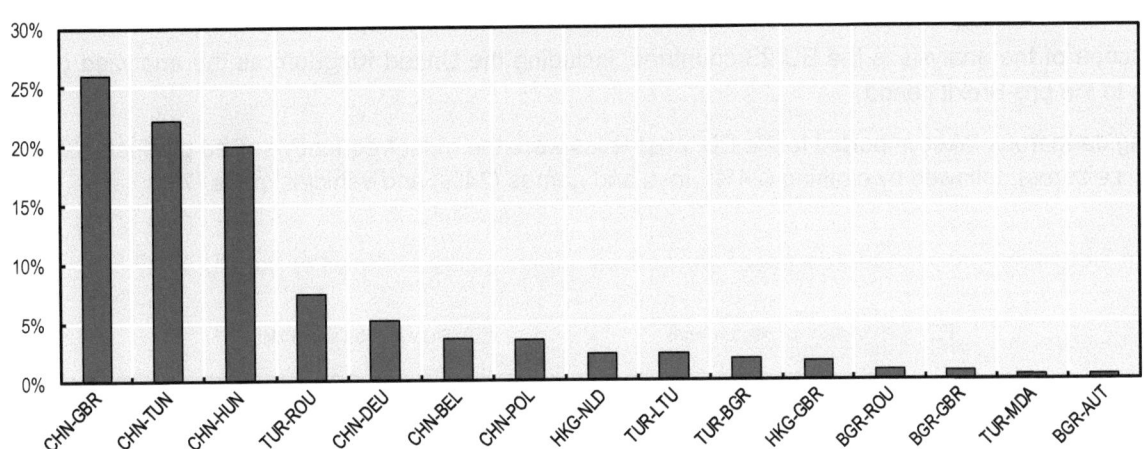

Source: OECD/EUIPO.

Figure 3.35 indicates that perfumes sent through small parcels were mostly sent via postal service as it represented almost 80% of global customs seizures of these products.

Figure 3.35. Transport modes of the most frequently faked product (perfumes) sent via small parcels, 2017-19

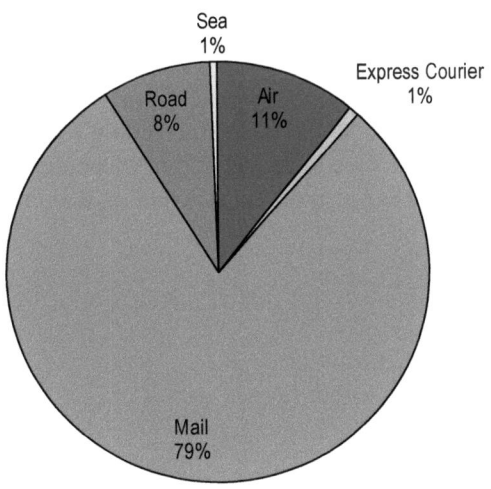

Source: OECD/EUIPO database.

EU Case Study

This section focuses on the trade of dangerous goods in European Union countries. It aims to provide information on the providers of dangerous fakes, and the most targeted countries in Europe, the most commonly counterfeited items, and the manner in which they are shipped to the European Union.

The scope of the analysis is the EU 28 countries, including the United Kingdom as the analyzed period refers to the pre-Brexit period.

Among dangerous fakes imported to the EU, cosmetics were the most frequently seized products (35% of global seizures), followed by clothing (24%), toys and games (24%) and vehicles' parts (7%).

Figure 3.36. Main product categories of dangerous fakes seized destined to the EU, 2017-19

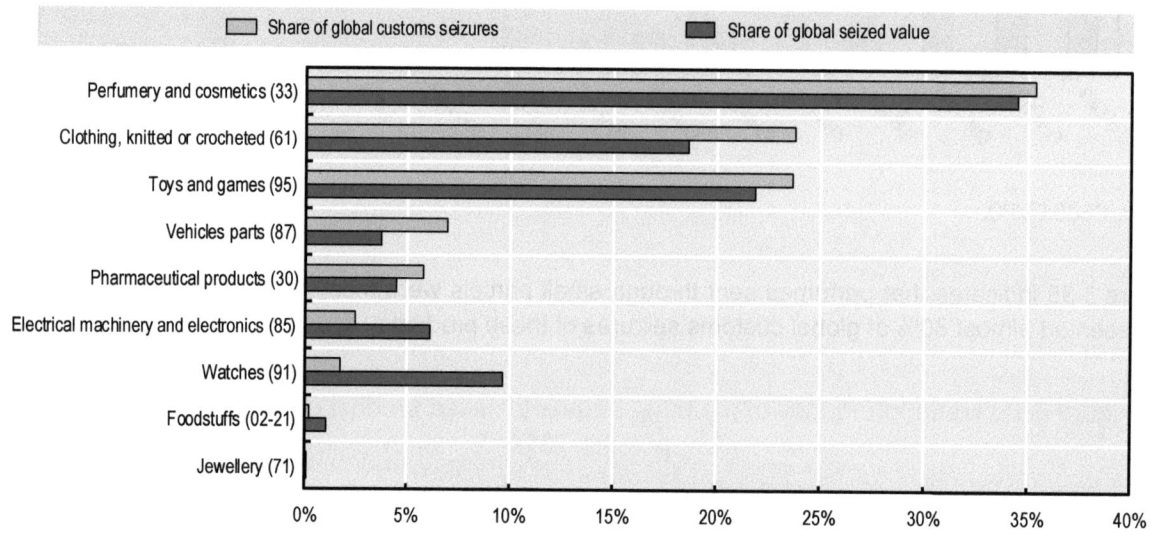

Source: OECD/EUIPO database.

Figure 3.37 shows that China, Hong Kong (China) and Turkey were the main source of dangerous fakes imported into the EU during 2017-19. Due to its geographical location, Turkey is a more important supplier of dangerous counterfeit goods in Europe than in the world as a whole.

Figure 3.37. Main provenance economies of dangerous fakes seized destined to the EU, 2017-19

[Bar chart showing Share of global customs seizures and Share of global seized value for: China (People's Republic of), Hong Kong (China), Turkey, Singapore, India, United States, Malaysia, Germany, Switzerland, Chinese Taipei*, Thailand, Russia, Nicaragua, Iran, Lebanon]

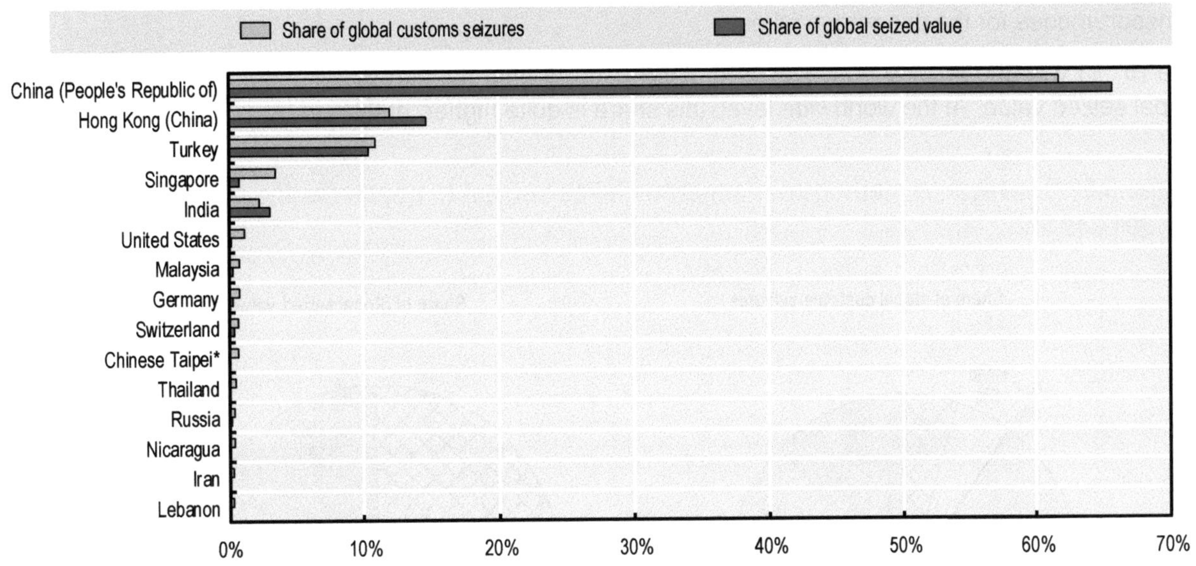

Source: OECD/EUIPO database.

Figure 3.38 which presents the main EU countries targeted by trade in dangerous fakes, indicates that Germany (47% of global customs seizures of dangerous fakes destined to EU) was by far the leading destination of these counterfeit goods during 2017-19. It was followed by Belgium, Denmark, Italy, Spain and Austria

The United Kingdom was the first European country targeted by trade in dangerous fakes in terms of seized value, receiving 26% of global seized value of dangerous fakes destined to the EU.

Figure 3.38. Main destination economies of dangerous fakes seized destined to the EU, 2017-19

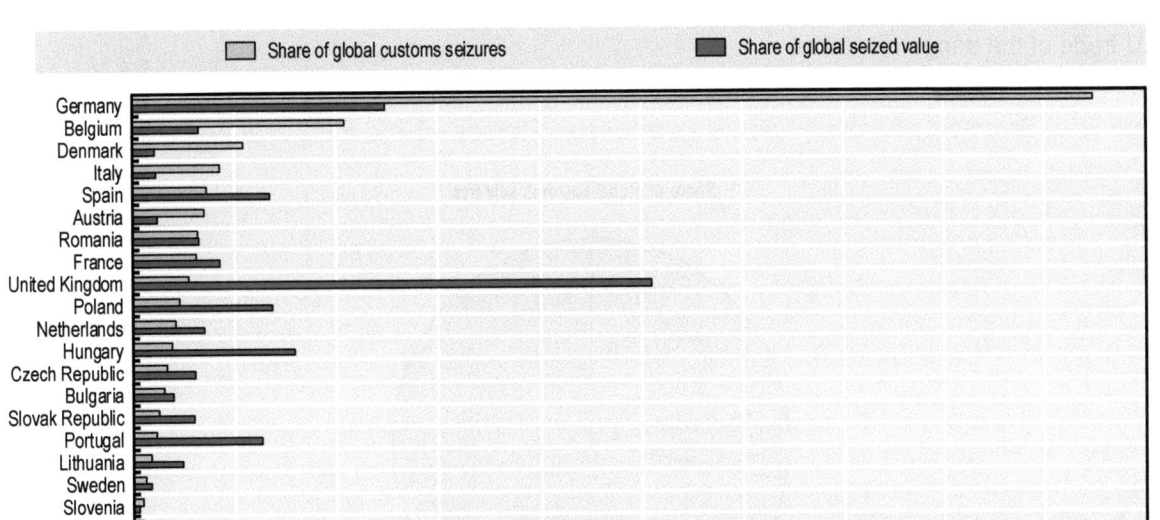

Source: OECD/EUIPO.

DANGEROUS FAKES © OECD/EUIPO 2022

Around 63% of global seizures of dangerous fakes destined for the EU were shipped by mail from 2017 to 2019 (see Figure 3.39). Express courrier (15%) and air (12%) were the other most frequently used transport modes for the dangerous fakes.

Sea (57%) was the leading conveyance method used to ship dangerous fakes into the EU in terms of global seized value. At the worldwide level, this share is quite higher, at 64%.

Figure 3.39. Conveyance methods of dangerous fakes subject to counterfeiting imported into the EU, 2017-19

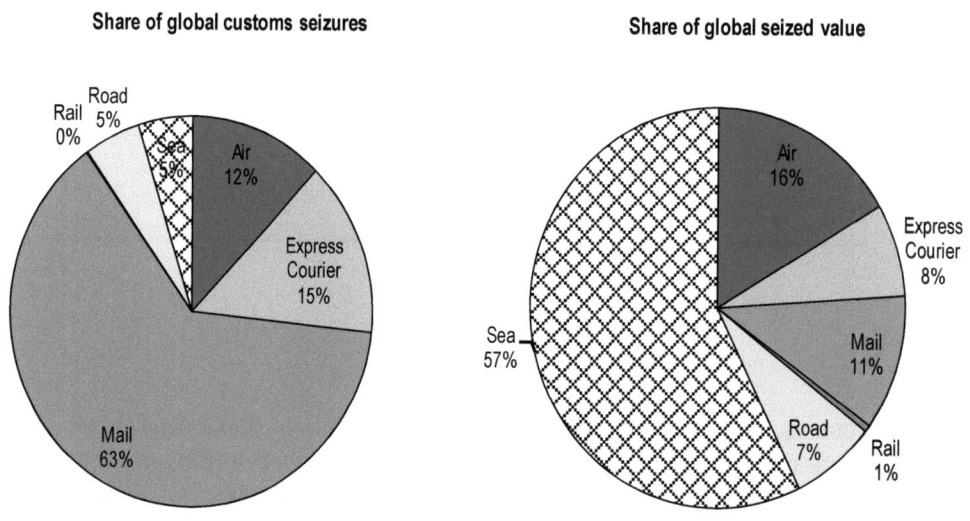

Source: OECD/EUIPO database.

Figure 3.40 indicates that the size of shipments of dangerous fakes seized destined to the EU tends to be small as 56% of seizures contained only one item from 2017 to 2019. Large shipments (i.e. more than 10 items) only concerned 22% of global seizures of dangerous fakes destined to the EU, while this share was higher at the worldwide level (36%). This trend is partly linked to the limited role of containerized shipments in EU trade of the dangerous fakes.

Figure 3.40. Shipment size of dangerous goods seized imported into the EU, 2017-19

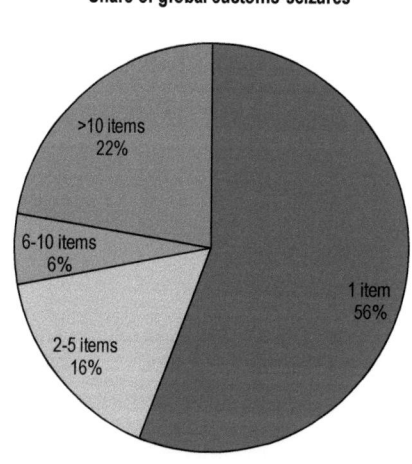

Source: OECD/EUIPO database

The role of e-commerce

Some seizures recorded by custom offices of the EU Member States contain information that they were related to online sales of goods. The link with online sale of goods is determined by custom officers on a case–by-case basis, taking documentation accompanying the shipped goods into account. In practice the collection and provision of online sales data is uneven among EU Member States. Whereas in some countries the majority of the detentions are associated with online sales, in other countries no single seizure has been associated with online sales of goods in the entire 2017-2019 period. To reduce the impact of this unevenness on the analysis, data from countries which do not report any detentions related to online sales or where the share of detentions related to online sales is lower than 5% have been eliminated from further analysis.

Among dangerous fakes destined to the EU, the majority of purchase were made online (see Figure 3.41). From 2017 to 2019, online sales represented 60% of global seizures of dangerous products destined to the EU. In terms of seized value, they only represented a small share (11% of global seized value).

Figure 3.41. Distribution of online and offline sales among dangerous fakes destined to the EU, 2017-19

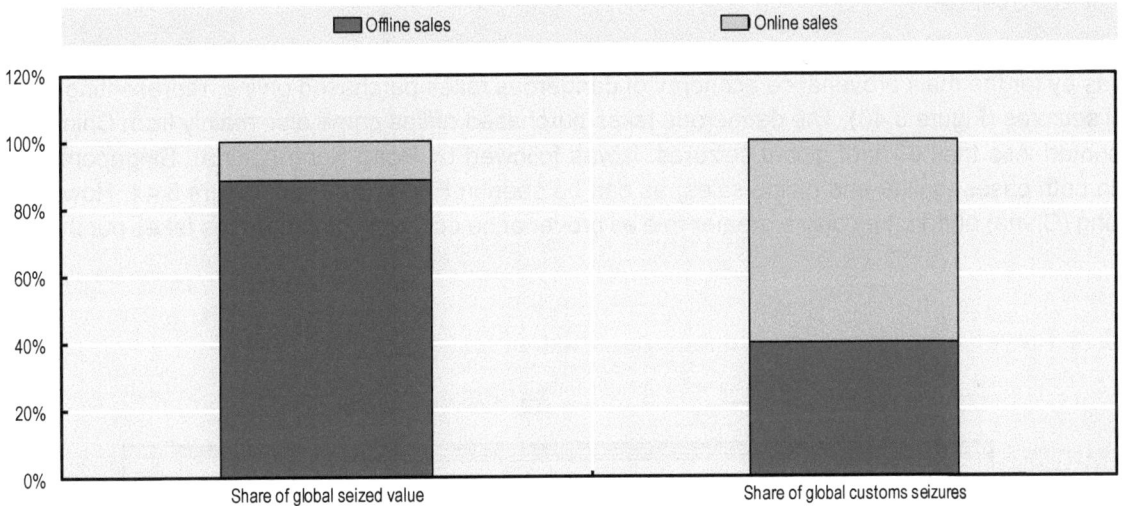

Source: OECD/EUIPO database

From 2017 to 2019, cosmetics were the most frequently seized products among dangerous fakes purchased online (see Figure 3.42). 46% of the purchase of dangerous fakes made online were cosmetics items, followed by clothing (18%), toys and games (17%) and automotive spare parts (8%).

Figure 3.42. Product categories of dangerous fakes purchased online, 2017-19

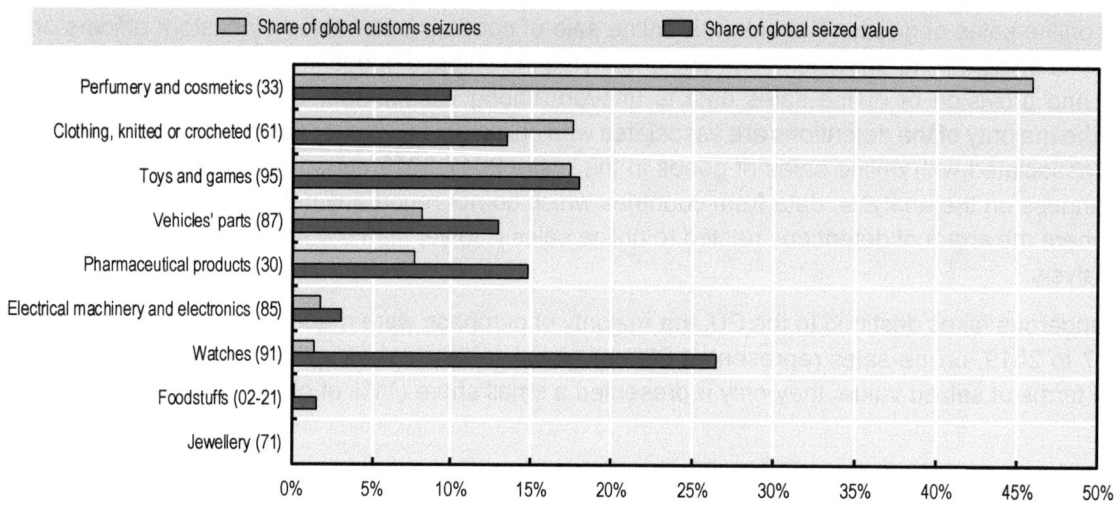

Source: OECD/EUIPO database.

China was by far the main provenance economy of dangerous fakes purchased online, representing 75% of global seizures (Figure 3.43). The dangerous fakes purchased offline came also mainly from China but it represented less than 60% of global seizures. It was followed by Hong Kong (China), Singapore and Turkey in both cases (online and offline sales) as can be seen in Figure 3.43 and Figure 3.44. However, Hong Kong (China) and Turkey play a greater role as provenance economy of dangerous fakes purchased offline.

Figure 3.43. Provenance economies of dangerous fakes purchased online, 2017-19

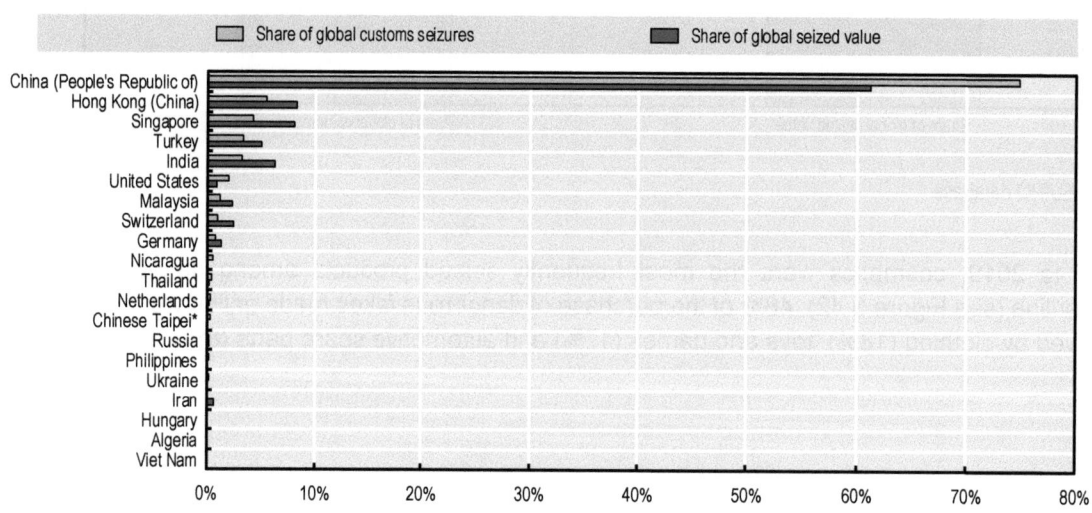

Source: OECD/EUIPO database.

Figure 3.44. Provenance economies of dangerous fakes purchased on site, 2017-19

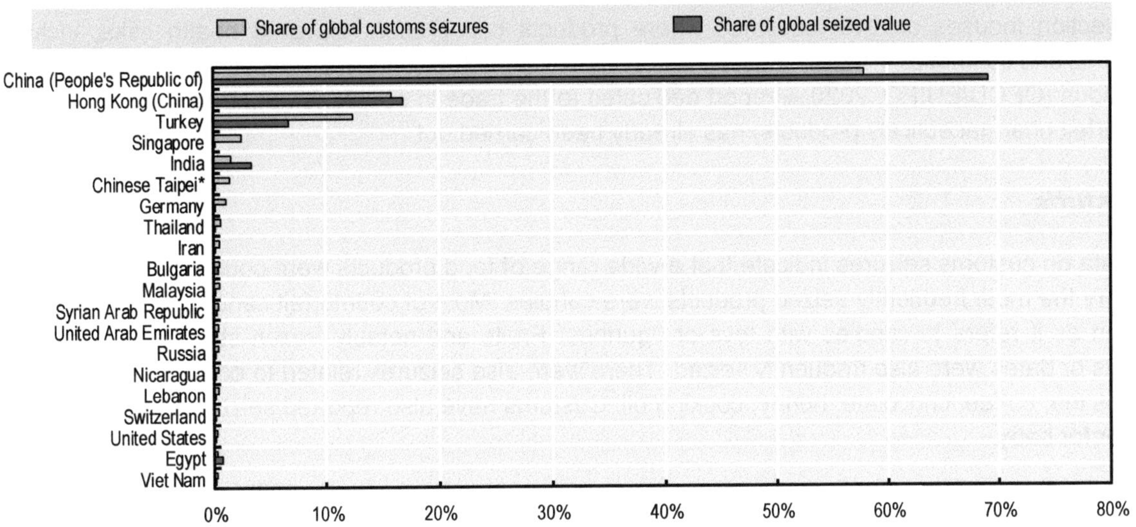

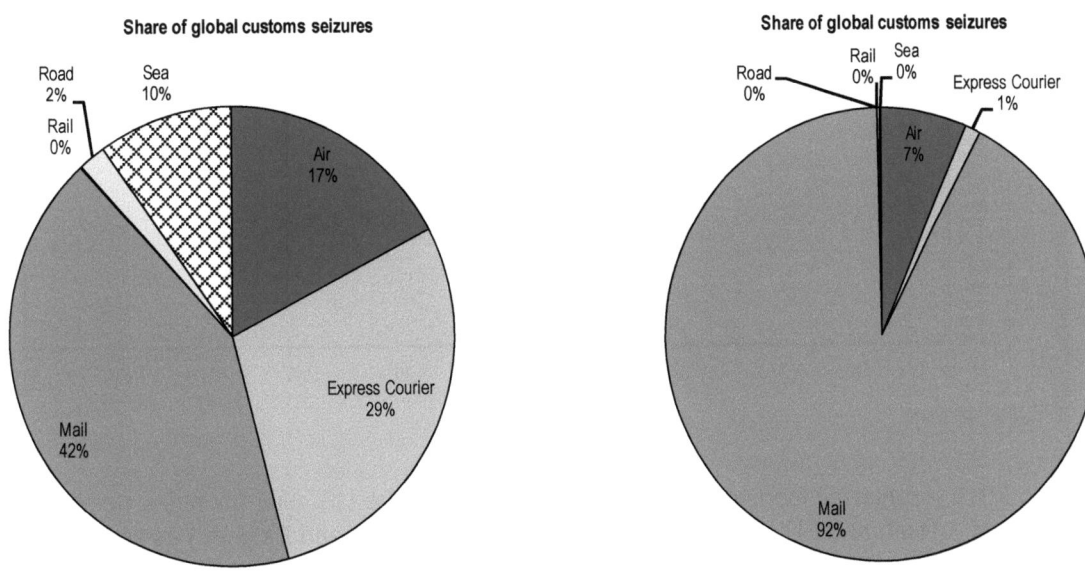

Source: OECD/EUIPO database.

The postal service dominates in terms of number of seizures, whether the sale of counterfeit goods has been performed online, or not. In the case of online sales however, mail is associated with 92% of seizures (compared to 42% of seizures of offline sales). All other modes of transport play a far lesser role in the online sale of counterfeit goods than in case of shipment of counterfeit goods not related to online sale. Air transport is the second most important transport mode associated with online sale of dangerous fakes (around 7% of seizures).

Figure 3.45. Modes of transport of dangerous fakes purchased on site (left) and online (right), 2017-19, in terms of number of global customs seizures

Source: OECD/EUIPO database

Industry focuses

This section focuses on two industries where products can present elevated health risks, including foodstuffs and cosmetics. Pharmaceuticals are also of high interest in the framework of this study, however a previous (OECD/EUIPO, 2020[26])report dedicated to the trade in counterfeit pharmaceuticals (Trade in counterfeit pharmaceuticals products) has already been carried out.

Foodstuffs

The data on customs seizures indicate that a wide range of food products were counterfeited. Within this category the most frequently seized products were candies. Most of counterfeit candies were destined to children as it refers to candies with toys or figurines. Fruits and notably frozen strawberries, oranges, apricots or dates were also frequently seized. There were also seizures related to common food products such as tea, coffee, chocolate, honey, cooking oil. Customs have also reported seizure of counterfeit milk powder for baby.

As can be seen in Figure 3.46, the leading provenance economies for counterfeit foodstuffs were China, Hong Kong (China) and Turkey. However, the Middle East countries played a greater role in trade in counterfeit foodstuffs than in global trade in fakes. Several Middle East countries were reported as provenance for fake foodstuffs, including United Arab Emirates, Egypt, Oman, Pakistan, Kuwait, Jordan, Syrian Arab Republic, Saudi Arabia and Bahrain.

Figure 3.46. Main provenance economies of counterfeit foodstuffs, 2017-19

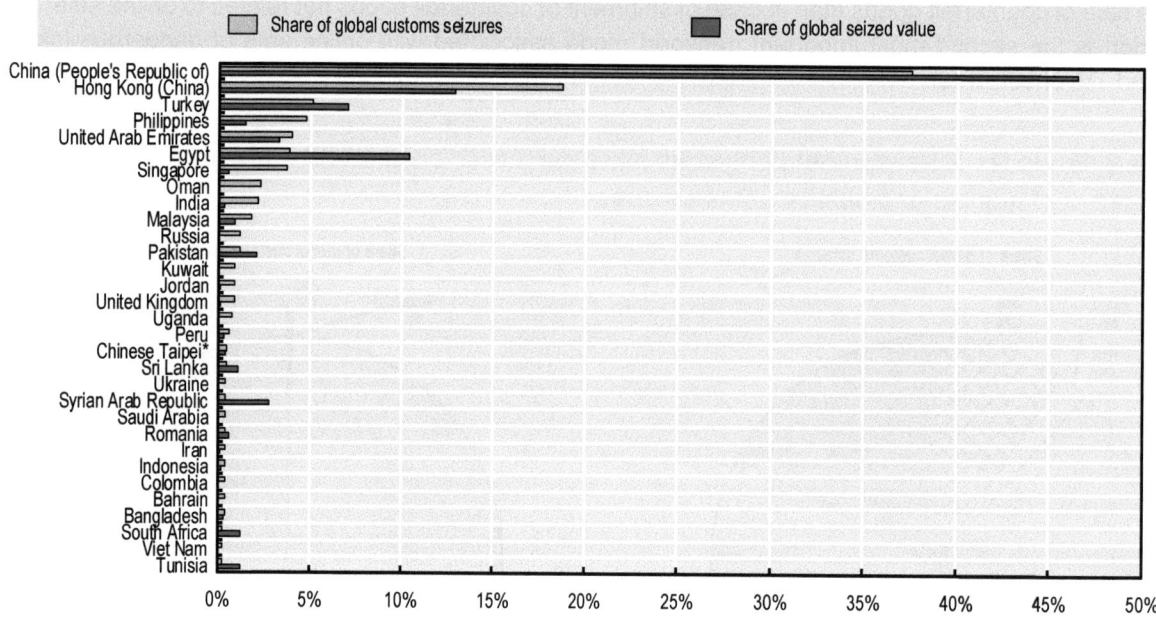

Source: OECD/EUIPO database.

From 2017 to 2019, counterfeit foodstuffs were mainly destined to the US, Gulf countries (led by Saudi Arabia, Qatar and Kuwait) and EU countries (led by Lithuania, Germany and Belgium) as can be seen in Figure 3.47. This indicates that within the Gulf region there were trade flows of counterfeit foodstuffs during 2017-19 period as these countries appeared both as provenance and destination.

Figure 3.47. Main destination economies of counterfeit foodstuffs, 2017-19

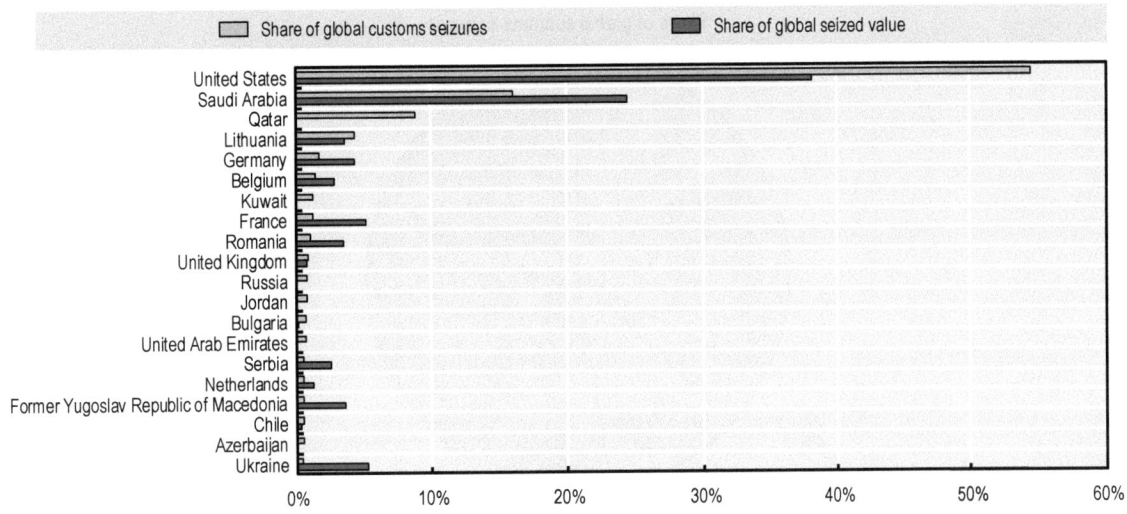

Source: OECD/EUIPO database.

While mail was usually the leading transport mode of counterfeit goods overall, sea was the preferred transport mode to ship counterfeit foodstuffs in terms of both the number of seizures and the global seized value from 2017 to 2019 (see Figure 3.48).

Figure 3.48. Transport modes used to ship counterfeit foodstuffs, 2017-19

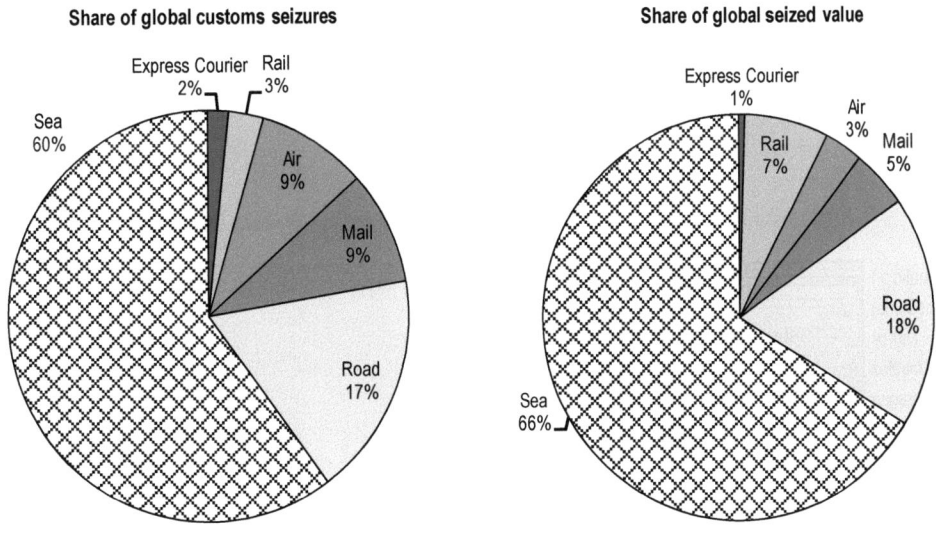

Source: OECD/EUIPO database.

Consequently, the average shipments size of counterfeit foodstuffs tended to be big. As can be seen in Figure 3.49, one third of seizures of counterfeit food products contained more than 1000 items.

DANGEROUS FAKES © OECD/EUIPO 2022

Figure 3.49. Shipments size of counterfeit food products, 2017-19

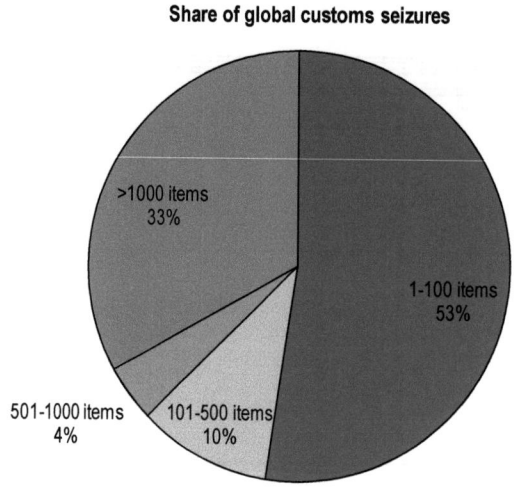

Source: OECD/EUIPO database.

Cosmetics

Within this category the most frequently intercepted products were perfumes from several brands. Make-up products (i.e. lipstick, bb cream, eyeshadow pallet, skin powder, etc) were also frequently seized by customs. There were around 23000 seizures of counterfeit cosmetics from 2017 to 2019.

Figure 3.50 shows that counterfeit cosmetics seized during 2017-19 originated from China (68%), Hong Kong (China) (15%), Turkey (8%) and United Arab Emirates (1%).

In terms of value, China (78% of global seized value) and India (11%) were the leading provenance economies of counterfeit perfumes and cosmetics.

Figure 3.50. Top provenance economies for counterfeit perfumery and cosmetics, 2017-19

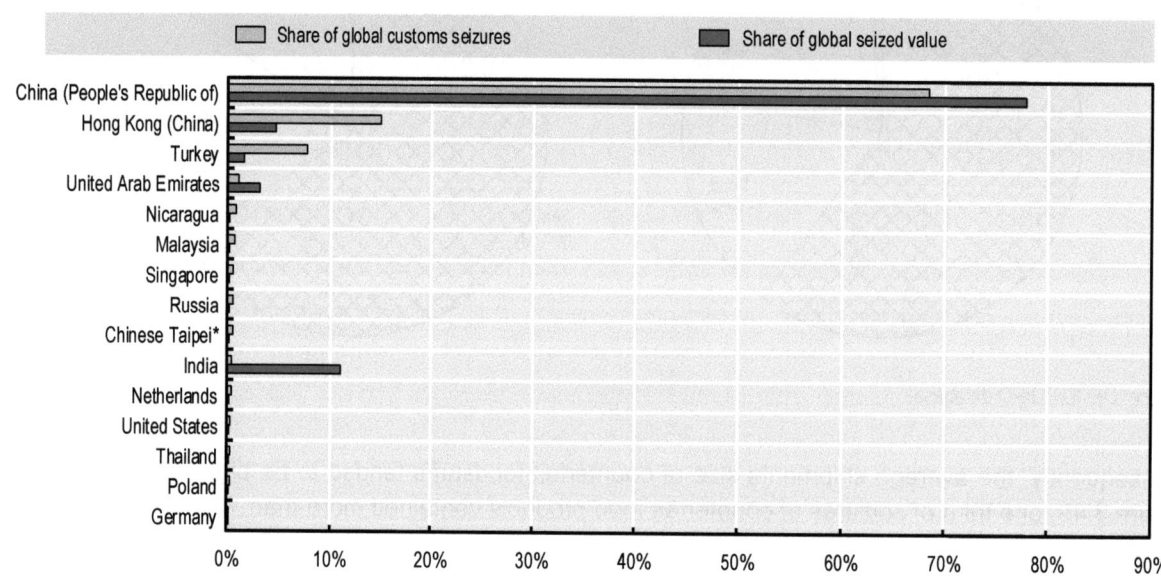

Source: OECD/EUIPO database

European countries and the US were the main destination economies for counterfeit perfumery and cosmetics from 2017 to 2019 (see Figure 3.51). Apart from these countries, Saudi Arabia was also included in the top destinations of counterfeit cosmetics, and accounted for 3% of global seized value of these products.

Figure 3.51. Top destination economies for counterfeit perfumery and cosmetics, 2017-19

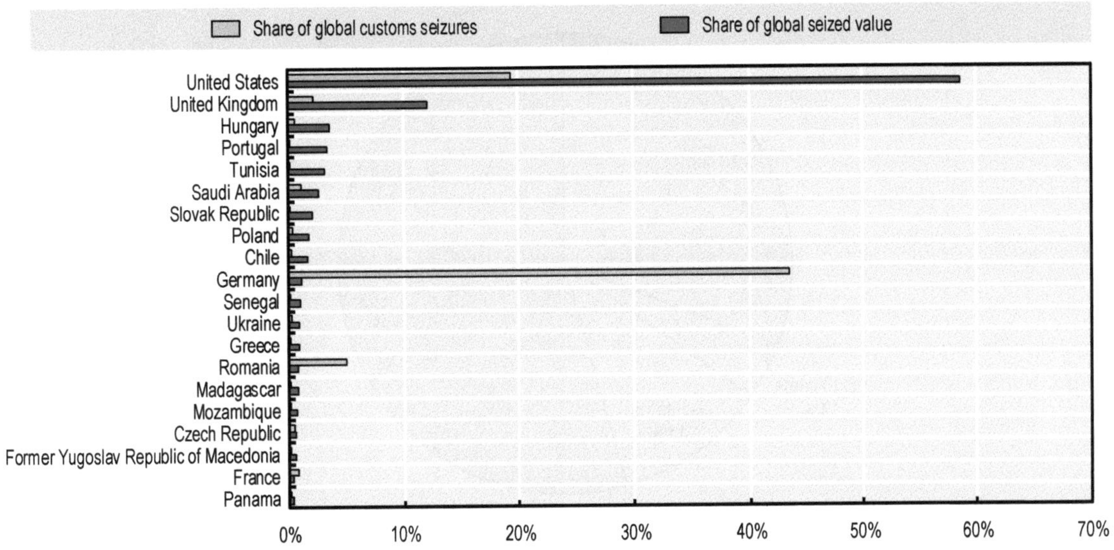

Source: OECD/EUIPO database.

Counterfeit perfumes and cosmetics were mostly shipped by mail which represented 77% of global seizures (see Figure 3.52). Road was the second transport mode for shipping counterfeit perfumery and cosmetics (equivalent to 10% of global seizures), followed by air (6%) and sea (4%).

In terms of global seized value, sea was by far the leading transport mode used to ship counterfeit cosmetics as it accounted for 81% of global seized value of these goods.

Figure 3.52. Conveyance methods used to ship counterfeit perfumery and cosmetics, 2017-19

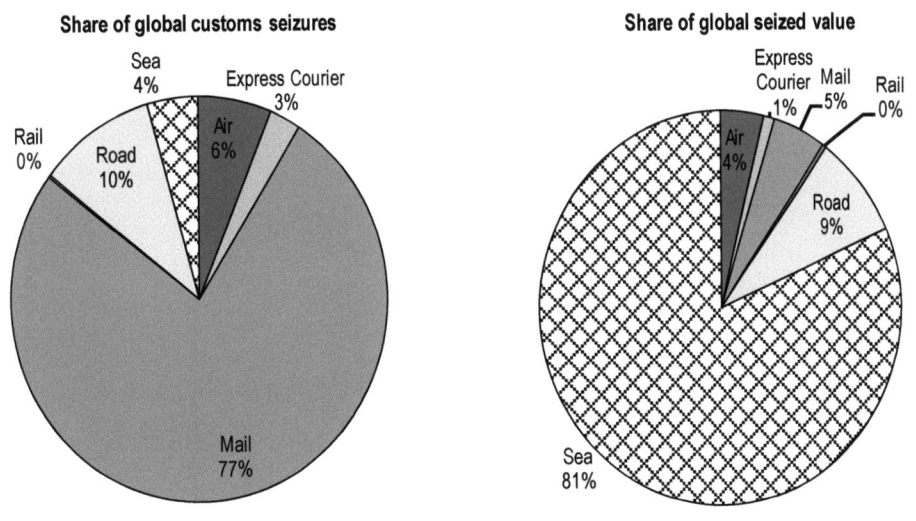

Source: OECD/EUIPO database.

DANGEROUS FAKES © OECD/EUIPO 2022

As postal service dominates in terms of shipping mode for counterfeit perfumery and cosmetics, the average size of shipment of these goods is small. Seizures of counterfeit perfumery and cosmetics containing only one item accounted for more than a half of total seizures (see Figure 3.53).

Figure 3.53. Shipment size of counterfeit perfumery and cosmetics, 2017-19

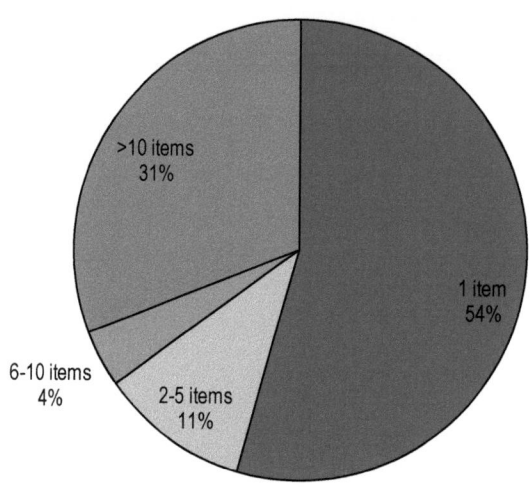

Source: OECD/EUIPO database.

4 Concluding Remarks

World trade continues to expand during the post-COVID recovery phase, bringing significant benefits to business and consumers alike, by providing them with opportunities to purchase a wide variety of goods at competitive prices from global suppliers. In the case of business, the development of global value chains has further enhanced the value of trade.

The revival of trade and continued efforts to lower barriers is an essential element of "building back better" policies. However, there are some risks related to the presence of illicit trade networks that pollute trade networks with counterfeit goods, generating significant health, safety and environmental threats.

Counterfeit goods have a wide range of negative consequences. Legitimate producers lose sales to counterfeiters, governments lose taxes and face corruption, while criminals thrive and expand illicit trade networks. This study highlights that in addition to these effects, counterfeits also can pose serious health, safety, environmental and other societal risks. Individuals who are unaware of the issue, can fall victim to low quality counterfeit products thereby threatening their health, and in some cases, their lives.

This study has analysed a unique international set of customs seizure data and other enforcement data, combining it with structured interviews with enforcement experts, to quantitatively assess the scope and trends of the trade in counterfeit products that can pose health, safety and environmental threats.

In terms of negative effects on health, this is particularly the case for counterfeit food, beverages, pharmaceuticals and related personal care items which have been improperly formulated or which contain ingredients that can be harmful. Such negative effects can ranging from mild inconveniences to consumers, to life-threatening situations. Moreover, in the case of pharmaceuticals, the lack of active ingredients can deprive consumers of the possibility to treat diseases effectively, thus prolonging illnesses that would otherwise be treatable.

Regarding the effects on safety, substandard counterfeit products raise serious safety concerns for a wide range of consumer products. Evidence provided by testing and certification bodies underscores that the volume of consumer products that can pose such risks (and are subject to testing and certification) is very broad, and includes toys, electronic devices, batteries, spare parts or household products.

Substandard counterfeit products often also have environmentally damaging consequences. Both the manufacture and the disposal of counterfeit items can have major impacts on the environment. In the manufacture of products, the use of toxic dyes, unlawful disposal of chemicals, and unregulated air pollution are problematic.

Importantly, many dangerous counterfeit products pose several risks at the same time. For example, a counterfeit pesticide can be harmful to the environment while at the same time posing health risks to people; fake spare parts (e.g. car battery) can pose safety and environmental risk; and a counterfeit medical device can pose both safety and health threats.

In addition, while some products could be considered relatively safe when they are manufactured, subsequent mishandling can pose problems. This is particularly the case for counterfeits and can happen for example, if goods are improperly stored or transported. For example products such as medicines often require transport and storage in special, temperature-controlled conditions in order to maintain their therapeutic value.

Of course the two sets: counterfeit goods and dangerous goods, are not perfectly overlapping. Some genuine products can also pose health, safety and environmental threats, which is why regulatory bodies are actively engaged in market surveillance. On the other hand absolute majority of fakes can pose some risks. This is because counterfeiters, have no incentives to meet any health, safety or environmental norms. While nearly all counterfeits are risky, some analytical approaches can be taken to take into account the varying degree of threats. Taking a broad approach that looks at all products that need to meet product specific health and safety requirements, before being placed on the market, one finds that apparel products, leather goods, electronics, watches and toys are the most frequently targeted products by counterfeiters.

A more focused approach that looks only at the most dangerous goods' categories: foodstuffs, pharmaceuticals, cosmetics and products that most frequently have been subject of alerts due to health, safety or environmental risks, reveals that the most commonly traded product categories of dangerous fakes were perfumery and cosmetics, clothing, toys, automotive spare parts and pharmaceuticals.

In all cases these goods come mostly from China and Hong Kong (China) that were identified as the main exporters of dangerous fakes accounting for more than three quarters of seizures.

Postal parcels – driven by the rising popularity of e-commerce – are the most popular ways of shipping counterfeit dangerous goods, significantly complicating the screening and detection processes and lowering the risk of detection and penalties. The EU countries and the United States were the main destination economies of the small parcels of dangerous goods. However, taking into account the value of the seizures, shipment by sea cargo clearly dominates; the distribution of destinations of dangerous fakes shipped by sea varied, with Gulf countries on top.

Importantly, online sales represented 60% of global seizures of dangerous products destined to the EU. In terms of seized value, they only represented a small share. In terms of dangerous fakes ordered online cosmetics items were on top, followed by clothing, toys and automotive spare parts.

The presence of dangerous counterfeit products also damages the value of the brand and image of the producers of genuine products over time. Effects of this sort were reported to several surveys as being linked to "erosion of company name" or "destruction of brand reputation". Such indications came from respondents across numerous sectors including consumer electronics, information and computers, electrical equipment, food and drink, luxury goods, sportswear, automotive spare parts and car accessories and pharmaceuticals (UKIPO, 2021[27]).

The COVID-19 pandemic has affected trade in dangerous fake goods, as it increased the demand of categories of products that are related to stronger health and safety standards and the original producers of those categories of goods were not able to quickly meet the higher demand. This is particularly the case for counterfeit medicines, and some other high-risk sectors such as food and alcohol, where broken supply chains and shifting demand opened new opportunities for criminals. However, the overall sharp increase in fakes concerned not only medicines and personal protective equipment (PPE) but many other goods that can also pose health and safety risks, including consumer goods and spare parts.

Health, safety and environmental risks posed by counterfeits are strong deterrents for consumers who consider purchasing counterfeit products. Consequently, precise and factual messaging on such risks could strengthen the awareness campaigns, and consequently reduce demand for fakes.

Next steps

With complex trade routes and increasingly sophisticated and flexible criminal networks, the health and safety threats posed by the counterfeit goods have become too complex to be addressed adequately by a single stakeholder, or a single country. The volume of risks posed by fakes to consumers, combined with the enormous scale of trade in counterfeits call for strengthening of international co-operation and a whole-of-governments approach.

Such approach should bring together a broad network of stakeholders from multiple countries, and from various sectors of government to foster international collaboration. Lessons learned from existing dedicated action, and special joint operations can provide examples of an effective international, whole-of-governments approach to a globally shared criminal threat. Still, more work is needed to deepen our understanding of many aspects of the issue – including regulatory frameworks, current trends, and technological challenges, the role of mail stream and free trade zones, and the need for approaches that combine multiple points of view and areas of expertise.

In addition, the quantitative analysis presented in this report identifies several research areas that might merit further investigation. A more in-depth analysis of these topics could be beneficial for developing efficient enforcement and governance frameworks to counter the risks posed by trade in counterfeit goods:

- Enhancing information collection. There are numerous examples of the adverse effects that counterfeit products can have on public health, safety and on the environment. These examples, however, have limited scope. A more systematic and extensive approach for developing data in this area is therefore needed. This could include application of specific systems on counterfeit medicine (see OECD/EUIPO, 2020) and their gradual adaptation towards other products. It could also include development of platforms for registering infringement-inflicted harm to consumers under public health disease classifications of unintentional injury.

- Examining governance and enforcement gaps. As highlighted by previous OECD/EUIPO studies, closing public governance and enforcement gaps are essential for effective action against illicit trade in counterfeits. Poor governance, corruption and weak intellectual property rights enforcement enable counterfeiters to misuse logistics and trade facilities. Some important provenance economies, where small parcels are very intensely used are characterised by seemingly sound governance and good quality infrastructure. It could be useful for policymakers to probe more deeply into why these economies play such important roles in trade in fake goods.

- Existing research indicates that illicit trade networks are dynamic. This is in addition complicated by the COVID-19 pandemic which has reinforced this dynamism. Further investigation into how these dynamics evolve is needed, either at the industry level or through a case-by-case analysis. This investigation should take into account the interplay between corruption, intellectual property enforcement gaps and the trade in dangerous fakes.

Annex A. Methodological notes

A.1. Constructing the General Trade-Related Index of Counterfeiting for products (GTRIC-p)

GTRIC-p is constructed through four steps:

1. For each reporting economy, the seizure percentages for sensitive goods are calculated.
2. For each product category, aggregate seizure percentages are calculated, taking the reporting economies' share of total sensitive imports as weights.
3. From these, a counterfeit source factor is established for each industry, based on the industries' weight in terms of total trade.
4. Based on these factors, the GTRIC-p is calculated.

Step 1: Measuring reporter-specific product seizure intensities

$\tilde{v}_i^k$ and $\tilde{m}_i^k$ are, respectively, the seizure and import values of product type *k* (as registered according to the HS on the two-digit level) in economy *i* from *any* provenance economy in a given year. Economy *i*'s relative seizure intensity (seizure percentages) of good *k*, denoted below as γ_i^k is then defined as:

$$\gamma_i^k = \frac{\tilde{v}_i^k}{\sum_{k=1}^{\bar{K}} \tilde{v}_i^k}, \text{ such that } \sum_{k=1}^{\bar{K}} \gamma_i^k = 1 \ \forall \ i \ \in \{1, \ldots, \bar{N}\}$$

$k = \{1, \ldots, \bar{K}\}$ is the range of sensitive goods (the total number of goods is given by *K*) and $i = \{1, \ldots, \bar{N}\}$ is the range of reporting economies (the total number of economies is given by *N*).

Step 2: Measuring general product seizure intensities

The general seizure intensity for product *k*, denoted Γ^k, is then determined by averaging seizure intensities, γ_i^k, weighted by the reporting economies' share of total sensitive imports in a given product category, *k*. Hence:

$$\Gamma^k = \sum_{i=1}^{\bar{N}} \omega_i \gamma_i^k , \ \forall \ k \ \in \{1, \ldots, \bar{K}\}$$

The weight of reporting economy i is given by:

$$\omega_i = \frac{\widetilde{m}_i^k}{\sum_{i=1}^{\overline{N}} \widetilde{m}_i^k}$$

where $\widetilde{m}_i$ is i's total registered import value of sensitive goods ($\sum_{i=1}^{\overline{n}} \omega_i = 1$)

Step 3: Measuring product-specific counterfeiting factors

$\widetilde{M}_i^k = \sum_{i=1}^{N} \widetilde{m}_i^k$ is defined as the total registered imports of sensitive good k for *all* economies and $\widetilde{M} = \sum_{k=1}^{\overline{K}} \widetilde{M}^k$ is defined as the total registered world imports of *all* sensitive goods.

The world import share of good k, denoted s^k, is therefore given by:

$$s^k = \frac{\widetilde{M}^k}{\widetilde{M}}, \text{ such that } \sum_{k=1}^{\overline{K}} s^k = 1$$

The general counterfeiting factor of product category k, denoted CP^k, is then determined as the following:

$$CP^k = \frac{\Gamma^k}{s^k}$$

The counterfeiting factor reflects the sensitivity of product infringements occurring in a particular product category, relative to its share in international trade. These are based on the seizure percentages calculated for each reporting economy and constitute the foundation of the formation of GTRIC-p.

Step 4: Establishing GTRIC-p

GTRIC-p is constructed from a transformation of the general counterfeiting factor and measures the relative likelihood that different product categories will be subject to counterfeiting and piracy in international trade. The transformation of the counterfeiting factor is based on two main assumptions:

- Assumption (A1): The counterfeiting factor of a particular product category is positively correlated with the actual intensity of international trade in counterfeit and pirated goods covered by that chapter. The counterfeiting factors must thus reflect the real intensity of actual counterfeit trade in the given product categories.
- Assumption (A2): This acknowledges that the assumption A1 may not be entirely correct. For instance, the fact that infringing goods are detected more frequently in certain categories could imply that differences in counterfeiting factors across products merely reflect that some goods are easier to detect than others or that some goods, for one reason or another, have been specially targeted for inspection. The counterfeiting factors of product categories with lower counterfeiting factors could, therefore, underestimate actual counterfeiting and piracy intensities in these cases.

In accordance with assumption A1 (positive correlation between counterfeiting factors and actual infringement activities) and assumption A2 (lower counterfeiting factors may underestimate actual activities), GTRIC-p is established by applying a positive monotonic transformation of the counterfeiting factor index using natural logarithms. This standard technique of linearisation of a non-linear relationship (in the case of this study between counterfeiting factors and actual infringement activities) allows the index to be flattened and gives a higher relative weight to lower counterfeiting factors (Verbeek, 2000[28]).

In order to address the possibility of outliers at both ends of the counterfeiting factor index (i.e. some categories may be measured as particularly susceptible to infringement even though they are not, whereas others may be measured as insusceptible although they are), it is assumed that GTRIC-p follows a left-truncated normal distribution, with GTRIC-p only taking values of zero or above.

The transformed counterfeiting factor is defined as:

$$cp^k = \ln(CP^k + 1)$$

Assuming that the transformed counterfeiting factor can be described by a left-truncated normal distribution with $cp^k \geq 0$, then, following Hald (Hald, 1952[29]), the density function of GTRIC-p is given by:

$$f_{LTN}(cp^k) = \begin{cases} 0 & \text{if } cp^k \leq 0 \\ \dfrac{f(cp^k)}{\int_0^\infty f(cp^k)dcp^k} & \text{if } cp^k \geq 0 \end{cases}$$

where $f(cp^k)$ is the non-truncated normal distribution for cp^k specified as:

$$f(cp^k) = \frac{1}{\sqrt{2\pi\sigma_{cp}^2}} \exp\left(-\frac{1}{2}\left(\frac{(cp^k) - \mu_{cp}}{\sigma_{cp}}\right)^2\right)$$

The mean and variance of the normal distribution, here denoted μ_{cp} and σ_{cp}^2, are estimated over the transformed counterfeiting factor index, cp^k, and given by $\hat{\mu}_{cp}^2$ and σ_{cp}^2. This enables the calculation of the counterfeit import propensity index (GTRIC-p) across HS codes, corresponding to the cumulative distribution function of cp^k.

A.2. Constructing the general trade-related index of counterfeiting economies (GTRIC-e)

GTRIC-e is also constructed through four steps:

1. For each reporting economy, the seizure percentages for provenance economies are calculated.
2. For each provenance economy, aggregate seizure percentages are calculated, taking the reporting economies' share of total sensitive imports as weights.
3. From these, each economy's counterfeit source factor is established, based on the provenance economies' weight in terms of total trade.
4. Based on these factors, the GTRIC-e is calculated.

Step 1: Measuring reporter-specific seizure intensities from each provenance economy

$\tilde{v}_i^j$ is economy i's registered seizures of all types of infringing goods (i.e. all k) originating from economy j in a given year in terms of their value. γ_i^j is economy i's relative seizure intensity (seizure percentage) of all infringing items that originate from economy j, in a given year:

$$\gamma_i^j = \frac{\tilde{v}_i^j}{\sum_{j=1}^{\bar{J}} \tilde{v}_i^j} \text{ such that } \sum_{j=1}^{\bar{J}} \gamma_i^j = 1 \ \forall \ i \in \{1, \ldots, \bar{N}\}$$

Where $j = \{1, ..., \bar{J}\}$ is the range of identified provenance economies (the total number of exporters is given by J) and $i = \{1, ..., \bar{N}\}$ is the range of reporting economies (the total number of economies is given by N).

Step 2: Measuring general seizure intensities of each provenance economy

The general seizure intensity for economy j, denoted Γ^j, is then determined by averaging seizure intensities, γ_i^j, weighted by the reporting economy's share of total imports from known counterfeit and pirate origins.[47] Hence:

$$\Gamma^j = \sum_{i=1}^{\bar{N}} \omega_i \gamma_i^j, \ \forall j \in \{1, ..., \bar{J}\}$$

The weight of reporting economy i is given by:

$$\omega_i = \frac{\widetilde{m}_i^j}{\sum_{i=1}^{\bar{N}} \widetilde{m}_i^j}, \text{ such that } \sum_{i=1}^{\bar{N}} \omega_i = 1$$

Step 3: Measuring partner-specific counterfeiting factors

$\bar{M}_i^j = \sum_{i=1}^{N} \widetilde{m}_i^j$ is defined as the total registered world imports of all sensitive products from j,[48] and $\bar{M} = \sum_{j=1}^{\bar{J}} \bar{M}^j$ is the total world import of sensitive goods from all provenance economies.

The share of imports from provenance economy j in total world imports of sensitive goods, denoted s^j, is then given by:

$$s^j = \frac{\bar{M}^j}{\bar{M}}, \text{ such that } \sum_{j=1}^{\bar{J}} s^j = 1$$

From this, the economy-specific counterfeiting factor is established by dividing the general seizure intensity for economy j by the share of total imports of sensitive goods from j.

$$CE^j = \frac{\Gamma^j}{s^j}$$

Step 4: Establishing GTRIC-e

Gauging the magnitude of counterfeiting and piracy from a provenance economy perspective can be done in a similar fashion as for sensitive goods. Hence, a General Trade-Related Index of Counterfeiting for economies (GTRIC-e) is established along similar lines and assumptions:

- Assumption (A3): The intensity by which any counterfeit or pirated article from a particular economy is detected and seized by customs is positively correlated with the actual amount of counterfeit and pirate articles imported from that location.
- Assumption (A4): This acknowledges that assumption A3 may not be entirely correct. For instance, a high seizure intensity of counterfeit or pirated articles from a particular provenance economy could be an indication that the provenance economy is part of a customs profiling scheme or that it is specially targeted for investigation by customs. The importance that provenance economies with low seizure intensities play regarding actual counterfeiting and piracy activity could, therefore, be under-represented by the index and lead to an underestimation of the scale of counterfeiting and piracy.

As with the product-specific index, GTRIC-e is established by applying a positive monotonic transformation of the counterfeiting factor index for provenance economies using natural logarithms. This follows from assumption A3 (positive correlation between seizure intensities and actual infringement activities) and assumption A4 (lower intensities tend to underestimate actual activities). Considering the possibilities of outliers at both ends of the GTRIC e-distribution (i.e. some economies may be wrongly measured as being particularly susceptible sources of counterfeit and pirated imports, and vice versa), GTRIC-e is approximated by a left-truncated normal distribution as it does not take values below zero.

The transformed general counterfeiting factor across provenance economies on which GTRIC-e is based is therefore given by applying logarithms onto economy-specific general counterfeit factors (see, for example, Verbeek (Verbeek, 2000[28])):

$$ce^j = ln(CE^j + 1)$$

In addition, following GTRIC-p, it is assumed that GTRIC-e follows a truncated normal distribution with $ce^j \geq 0$ for all j. Following Hald (Hald, 1952[29]), the density function of the left-truncated normal distribution for ce^j is given by:

$$g_{LTN}(ce^j) = \begin{cases} 0 & \text{if } ce^j \leq 0 \\ \dfrac{g(ce^j)}{\int_0^\infty g(ce^j)dce} & \text{if } ce^j \geq 0 \end{cases}$$

where $g(ce^j)$ is the non-truncated normal distribution for ce^j specified as:

$$g(ce^j) = \frac{1}{\sqrt{2\pi\sigma_{ce}^2}} exp\left(-\frac{1}{2}\left(\frac{ce^j - \mu_{ce}}{\sigma_{ce}}\right)^2\right)$$

The mean and variance of the normal distribution, here denoted μ_{ce} and σ_{ce}^2, are estimated over the transformed counterfeiting factor index, ce^j, and given by $\hat{\mu}_{ce}$ and $\hat{\sigma}_{ce}^2$. This enables the calculation of the counterfeit import propensity index (GTRIC-e) across provenance economies, corresponding to the cumulative distribution function of ce^j.

A.3. Constructing the General Trade-Related Index of Counterfeiting (GTRIC)

In the (OECD/EUIPO, 2016[2]) and (OECD/EUIPO, 2019[3]) studies, propensities to import infringing goods from different trading partners were developed using seizure data as a basis. The use of data is maximised by applying a generalised approach in which the propensities for products to be counterfeit and for economies to be sources of counterfeit goods were analysed separately. This increased the data coverage of both products and provenance economies significantly, which increases the robustness of the overall estimation results. Unfortunately, it also reduced the detail of the analysis, meaning that counterfeit trade patterns specific to individual reporting economies, for both product types and trading partners, were not simultaneously accounted for; this introduced bias into the results. On balance, however, given the large scope of the analysis, the advantages of increasing data coverage can be viewed as outweighing the biases.

This approach combines the two indices: GTRIC-p and GTRIC-e. In this regard, it is important to emphasise that the index resulting from this combination does not account for differences in infringement intensities across different types of goods that may exist between economies. For instance, imports of certain counterfeit and pirated goods could be particularly large from some trading partners and small from others. An index taking such "infringement specialisation", or concentration, into account is desirable and possible to construct; but it would require detailed seizure data. The combined index, denoted GTRIC, is, therefore, a generalised index that approximates the relative likelihoods that particular product types, imported from specific trading partners, are counterfeit and/or pirated.

Establishing likelihoods for product and provenance economy

In this step, for each trade flow from a given provenance economy and for a given product category the likelihoods of containing counterfeit and pirated products will be established.

The general propensity for an economy to export infringed items of HS category k is denoted P^k, and given by GTRIC-p, so that:

$$P^k = F_{LTN}(cp^k)$$

where $F_{LTN}(cp^k)$ is the cumulative probability function of $f_{LTN}(cp^k)$.

Furthermore, the general likelihood of importing any type of infringing goods from economy j is denoted as P^j, and given by GTRIC-e, so that:

$$P^j = G_{LTN}(ce^j)$$

where $G_{LTN}(ce^j)$ is the cumulative probability function of $f_{LTN}(ce^j)$.

The general probability of importing counterfeit or pirated items of type k originating from economy j is then denoted P^{jk} and approximated by:

$$P^{jk} = P^k P^j$$

Therefore, $P^{jk} \in [\varepsilon_p \varepsilon_e; 1)$, $\forall j, k$, with $\varepsilon_p \varepsilon_e$ denoting the minimum average counterfeit export rate for each sensitive product category and each provenance economy,[49] it is assumed that $\varepsilon_p = \varepsilon_e = 0.05$.

A.4. Calculating the absolute value

α is the fixed point, i.e. the maximum average counterfeit import rate of a given type of infringing good, k, originating from a given trading partner, j.

α can be applied to propensities for importing infringing goods of type j from trading partner k (αP^{jk}). As a result, a matrix of counterfeit import propensities **C** is obtained.

$$C = \begin{pmatrix} \alpha P^{11} & \alpha P^{21} & & & \alpha P^{1K} \\ \alpha P^{12} & \ddots & & & \\ \vdots & & \alpha P^{jk} & & \vdots \\ & & & \ddots & \\ \alpha P^{J1} & & & & \alpha P^{JK} \end{pmatrix} \text{ with dimension } J \times K$$

The matrix of world imports is denoted by **M**. Applying **C** on **M** yields the absolute volume of trade in counterfeit and pirated goods.

In particular, the import matrix **M** is given by:

$$M = \begin{pmatrix} M_1 \\ \vdots \\ M_i \\ \vdots \\ M_n \end{pmatrix} \text{ with dimension } n \times J \times K$$

Each element is defined by economy i's unique import matrix of good k from trading partner j.

$$M_i = \begin{pmatrix} m_{i1}^1 & m_{i1}^2 & & m_{i1}^K \\ m_{i2}^1 & \ddots & & \\ \vdots & & m_{ij}^k & \vdots \\ & & & \ddots \\ m_{iJ}^1 & & & m^{JK} \end{pmatrix} \text{ with dimension } J \times K$$

Hence, the element m_{ij}^k denotes i's imports of product category k from trading partner j, where $i = \{1, \ldots, n\}$, $j = \{1, \ldots, J\}$, and $k = \{1, \ldots, K\}$.

Denoted by Ψ, the product-by-economy percentage of counterfeit and pirated imports can be determined as the following:

$$\Psi = C'M \div M$$

Total trade in counterfeit and pirated goods, denoted by the scalar **TC**, is then given by:

$$TC = i_1' \Psi i_2$$

where i_1 is a vector of one with dimension $nJ \times 1$, and i_2 is a vector of one with dimension $K \times 1$. Then, by denoting total world trade by the scalar $TM = i_1' M i_2$, the value of counterfeiting and piracy in world trade, s_{TC}, is determined by:

$$s_{TC} = \frac{TC}{TM}$$

References

BSA (2016), *BSA Survey: Unlicensed Software Use Still High Globally, Despite Costly Cybersecurity Threats*, https://www.bsa.org/fr/node/35056. [24]

CPSC (n.d.), *CPSC Safety Alert*, http://www.cpsc.gov/s3fs-public/Hoverboard-Safety-Alert.pdf?mSAM5F_iz1JtmMI8UvtzohHxB6xSqARX. [18]

EUIPO (2019), *Qualitative study on risks posed by counterfeits to consumers*, https://euipo.europa.eu/tunnel-web/secure/webdav/guest/document_library/observatory/documents/reports/2019_Risks_Posed_by_Counterfeits_to_Consumers_Study/2019_Risks_Posed_by_Counterfeits_to_Consumers_Study.pdf. [8]

EUIPO (2016), *The economic cost of IPR infringement in the spirits and wine sector*, European Union Intellectual Property Office, Alicante, https://euipo.europa.eu/tunnel-web/secure/webdav/guest/document_library/observatory/resources/research-and-studies/ip_infringement/study8/wines_and_spirits_en.pdf. [30]

FDA (n.d.), *Recalls, Market Withdrawals, & Safety Alerts*, http://www.fda.gov/safety/recalls-market-withdrawals-safety-alerts. [6]

Frankel, T. (2019), *Number of children swallowing dangerous magnets surges as industry largely polices itself*, https://www.washingtonpost.com/business/economy/number-of-children-swallowing-dangerous-magnets-surges-as-industry-largely-polices-itself/2019/12/25/77327812-2295-11ea-86f3-3b5019d451db_story.html. [17]

Hald, A. (1952), *Statistical Theory with Engineering Applications*, John Wiley and Sons, New York. [29]

Holland, K. (2020), *Counterfeit Makeup a Rip-Off... and a Health Danger*, https://www.healthline.com/health-news/counterfeit-makeup-a-health-danger. [13]

IATA (2021), *2021 Lithium Battery Guidance Document - Transport of Lithium Metal and Lithium Ion Batteries*, https://www.iata.org/contentassets/05e6d8742b0047259bf3a700bc9d42b9/lithium-battery-guidance-document-2021.pdf. [19]

IDC (2013), *The dangerous world of counterfeit and pirated software*, https://news.microsoft.com/download/presskits/antipiracy/docs/IDC030513.pdf. [25]

Kent, M. (2020), *Taking Fake Toys Offline: A 2020 Focus on Proactive Measures to Reduce Counterfeits and Unsafe Toys Sold on Online Marketplaces*, https://www.toyassociation.org/App_Themes/toyassociation_resp/downloads/research/whitepapers/FakeToys-WhitePaper.pdf. [16]

Lachenmeier Dirk W. Maria Neufeld and Jürgen Rehm (2021), *The Impact of Unrecorded Alcohol Use on Health: What Do We Know in 2020?*, Journal of Studies on Alcohol and Drugs, https://doi.org/10.15288/jsad.2021.82.28. [12]

Metzler, A. (2011), *NIOSH Fact Sheet: NIOSH Approval Labels—Key Information to Protect Yourself*, https://www.cdc.gov/niosh/docs/2011-179/. [21]

NHSTA (n.d.), *Safety Issues & Recalls*, http://www.nhtsa.gov/recalls. [7]

OECD (n.d.), *GlobalRecalls*, https://globalrecalls.oecd.org/. [5]

OECD/EUIPO (2020), *Trade in Counterfeit Pharmaceutical Products*, Illicit Trade, OECD Publishing, Paris, https://dx.doi.org/10.1787/a7c7e054-en. [26]

OECD/EUIPO (2019), *Trends in Trade in Counterfeit and Pirated Goods*, Illicit Trade, OECD Publishing, Paris/European Union Intellectual Property Office, Alicante, https://dx.doi.org/10.1787/g2g9f533-en. [3]

OECD/EUIPO (2016), *Trade in Counterfeit and Pirated Goods: Mapping the Economic Impact*, Illicit Trade, OECD Publishing, Paris, https://dx.doi.org/10.1787/9789264252653-en. [2]

OECD/EUIPO (2021b), *Global Trade in Fakes: a Worrying Threat*, OECD Publishing, https://www.oecd.org/publications/global-trade-in-fakes-74c81154-en.htm. [1]

Rahman, E. (2018), *The health consequences of falsified medicines- A study of the published literature*, https://doi.org/10.1111/tmi.13161. [11]

Renschler et al. (2015), *Estimated under-five deaths associated with poor-quality antimalarials in sub-Saharan Africa*, http://dx.doi.org/10.4269/ajtmh.14-0725. [10]

TRACIT (n.d.), *Counterfeit products with health and safety implications*, http://www.tracit.org/uploads/1/0/2/2/102238034/counterfeit_products_with_health_and_safety_implications_9_29_21.pdf. [4]

UKIPO (2021), *Counterfeit Goods Research – Wave 2*, https://assets.publishing.service.gov.uk/government/uploads/system/uploads/attachment_data/file/1041630/Physical-Goods-Wave2.pdf. [27]

UL (2021), *Anti-Counterfeiting Virtual Research Symposium*, https://ul.org/research/anti-counterfeiting/anti-counterfeiting-virtual-research-symposium. [23]

UL (2020), *Brand Protection 2019 Year in Review*, https://www.ul.com/sites/g/files/qbfpbp251/files/2020-07/2019%20GSBP%20Annual%20Report_EN_web.pdf. [14]

UL (2020), *Counterfeit iPhone adapters*, https://besafebuyreal.ul.org/sites/default/files/2020-11/CS12371_Apple_Counterfeit%20Iphone%20Adapters_WP_LR.pdf. [20]

UL (n.d.), *Public Notices*, http://www.ul.com/news/public-notices. [15]

Verbeek, M. (2000), *A Guide to Modern Econometrics*, Wiley. [28]

WHO (2021), *Global alcohol action plan 2022-2030 to strengthen implementation of the Global Strategy to Reduce the Harmful Use of Alcohol,*, World Health Organization, Geneva, http://www.who.int/publications/m/item/global-action-plan-on-alcohol-1st-draft. [31]

WHO (2017), *1 in 10 medical products in developing countries is substandard or falsified*, https://www.who.int/news/item/28-11-2017-1-in-10-medical-products-in-developing-countries-is-substandard-or-falsified. [9]

WIPO (2017), *The environmentally safe disposal and destruction of intellectual property infringing goods*, https://www.wipo.int/edocs/mdocs/enforcement/en/wipo_ace_12/wipo_ace_12_3_rev.pdf. [22]

Notes

[1] See www.ice.gov/features/dangers-counterfeit-items.

[2] See: https://euipo.europa.eu/tunnel-web/secure/webdav/guest/document_library/observatory/documents/reports/2019_Risks_Posed_by_Counterfeits_to_Consumers_Study/2019_Risks_Posed_by_Counterfeits_to_Consumers_Study.pdf

[3] Regulation (EC) No 765/2008 of the European Parliament and of the Council of 9 July 2008 setting out the requirements for accreditation and market surveillance relating to the marketing of products and repealing Regulation (EEC) No 339/93 and Decision No 768/2008/EC of the European Parliament and of the Council of 9 July 2008 on a common framework for the marketing of products, and repealing Council Decision 93/465/EEC

[4] Regulation (EU) 2019/1020 of the European Parliament and of the Council of 20 June 2019 on market surveillance and compliance of products and amending Directive 2004/42/EC and Regulations (EC) No 765/2008 and (EU) No 305/2011, started to apply on 16 July 2021.

[5] There are more than 20 pieces of EU legislation aligned with the NLF. The areas concerned are toys; measuring instruments; recreational craft and personal watercraft; low voltage equipment; radio equipment; civil explosives; simple pressure vessels; medical devices; personal protective equipment; gas appliances; EU fertiling products.

[6] https://legalinstruments.oecd.org/en/instruments/OECD-LEGAL-0459

[7] This is the case for instance of the General Product Safety Directive applicable in the European Union (Directive 2001/95/EC of the European Parliament and of the Council of 3 December 2001 on general product safety).

[8] References to harmonised standards and other European standards published in the OJEU can be found on the webpage https://ec.europa.eu/growth/single-market/european-standards/harmonised-standards_en

[9] See www.congress.gov/bill/117th-congress/house-bill/3429.

[10] See www.congress.gov/bill/116th-congress/house-bill/6058.

[11] The associations include the Alliance for Safe Online Pharmacies, Automotive Anti-Counterfeiting Council, American Apparel & Footwear Association,, Association of Home Appliance Manufacturers, Communications Cable & Connectivity Association, Consumer Healthcare Products Association, Halloween Industry Association, Juvenile Products Manufacturers Association, Natural Products Association, Personal Care Products Council, TIC Council Americas, Toy Association, and Transnational Association to Combat Illicit Trade.

[12] See www.aafaglobal.org/AAFA/AAFA_News/2021_Letters_and_Comments/Multi_Association_Letter_in_Support_of_SHOP_SAFE_Act.aspx.

[13] See www.tracit.org/uploads/1/0/2/2/102238034/tracit_written_statement_on_h_shop_safe_act_may_27_2020.pdf.

[14] See www.americanbar.org/content/dam/aba/administrative/intellectual_property_law/advocacy/aba-ipl-comments-on-shop-safe-act-final.pdf.

[15] See https://globalrecalls.oecd.org/.

[16] Where complete information is not available in cases involving serious risk, a "Notification for information" can also be made under the Safety Gate system.

[17] Reporting the possible counterfeit character of products subject to notifications under Safety Gate is relatively low as notifying authorities often do not have the necessary information to identify fakes. Moreover, counterfeit products are, as a rule, destroyed when they are seized, generally without safety testing by national authorities.

[18] See https://buysaferx.pharmacy//wp-content/uploads/2020/06/Patient-Harms-Tracker-6-4-2020.pdf.

[19] See www.incoproip.com/reports/counterfeit-products-are-destroying-brand-value/.

[20] See www.dailymail.co.uk/health/article-2312986/Sarah-Houston-Banned-slimming-drug-DNP-kills-medical-student-coroner-attacks-online-dealers-target-vulnerable.html.

[21] See www.dea.gov/press-releases/2021/09/27/dea-issues-public-safety-alert.

[22] See www.fbi.gov/news/stories/counterfeit-cosmetics-fragrances.

[23] See www.bbc.com/news/uk-45313747.

[24] See www.amcostarica.com/Alert%20on%20two%20versions%20of%20fake%20Colgate%20toothpaste.html.

[25] See www.fda.gov/media/72959/download.

[26] See www.ice.gov/features/dangers-counterfeit-items.

[27] Argentina, Australia, Austria, Belgium, Canada, Chile, China, Colombia, France, Germany, Hong Kong (China), Ireland, Italy, Japan, Malaysia, Netherlands, Philippines, Poland, Portugal, Singapore, Spain, Switzerland, Thailand, United Kingdom and United States.

[28] See www.ul.com/news/ul-cracks-down-deceptive-practices-combat-fraudulent-personal-protective-equipment.

[29] See www.thesun.co.uk/money/10497431/dangerous-christmas-presents-fake-lol-surprise-toys/.

[30] See https://edition.cnn.com/2019/12/20/tech/amazon-fake-kids-products/index.html.

[31] See www.ul.com/news/ul-teams-law-enforcement-brand-defense.

[32] See https://electronics360.globalspec.com/article/17110/counterfeit-part-rise-will-linger-through-2023.

[33] See www.semiconductors.org/wp-content/uploads/2018/06/ACTF-Whitepaper-Counterfeit-One-Pager-Final.pdf.

[34] See www.semiconductors.org/how-to-stop-counterfeit-semiconductors/.

[35] See https://electronics360.globalspec.com/article/17259/the-growing-danger-of-counterfeit-batteries.

[36] Off-nominal conditions occur when elements of the system are operating as designed, but operational or environmental factors are not as planned or as forecast.

[37] See www.smh.com.au/national/nsw/faulty-usb-phone-charger-blamed-for-sheryl-aldeguers-death-20140627-zsoc8.html.

[38] See https://www.grandviewresearch.com/industry-analysis/aftermarket-automotive-parts-market.

[39] See https://docs.house.gov/meetings/JU/JU03/20190718/109812/HHRG-116-JU03-Wstate-CammisoJ-20190718.pdf.

[40] See https://iipcic.org/courseSamples/A2C2/EN/presentation_content/external_files/A2C2%20Brochure.pdf.

[41] See www.incoproip.com/counterfeit-car-parts-risking-lives/.

[42] See www.tractionnews.com/be-aware-of-counterfeit-tires.

[43] See www.cdc.gov/niosh/npptl/topics/respirators/disp_part/n95list1.html.

[44] See www.cdc.gov/niosh/npptl/usernotices/counterfeitResp.html.

[45] See www.cdc.gov/coronavirus/2019-ncov/prevent-getting-sick/types-of-masks.html.

[46] See www.microsoft.com/security/blog/2018/04/02/take-these-steps-to-stay-safe-from-counterfeit-software-and-fraudulent-subscriptions/.

[47] This is different to the economy's share of total imports of sensitive goods used to calculate GTRIC-p.

[48] This is different to the total imports of sensitive goods as used in calculation of GTRIC-p.

[49] In the OECD methodology, these factors were applied to all provenance economies and all HS modules in order to account for counterfeit and pirated exports of products and/or from provenance economies that were not identified.

Printed by Libri Plureos GmbH in Hamburg,
Germany